A Million Words and Counting

A Million Words and Counting

HOW GLOBAL ENGLISH IS REWRITING THE WORLD

Paul J. J. Payack

CITADEL PRESS
Kensington Publishing Corp.
www.kensingtonbooks.com

CITADEL PRESS BOOKS are published by

Kensington Publishing Corp.
850 Third Avenue
New York, NY 10022

All Kensington titles, imprints, and distributed lines are available at special quantity discounts for bulk purchases for sales promotions, premiums, fund-raising, educational, or institutional use. Special book excerpts or customized printings can also be created to fit specific needs. For details, write or phone the office of the Kensington special sales manager: Kensington Publishing Corp., 850 Third Avenue, New York, NY 10022, attn: Special Sales Department; phone 1-800-221-2647.

CITADEL PRESS and the Citadel logo are Reg. U.S. Pat. & TM Off.

First printing: May 2008

10 9 8 7 6 5 4 3 2 1

Printed in the United States of America

Library of Congress Control Number: 2007928706

ISBN-13: 978-0-8065-2857-1

ISBN-10: 0-8065-2857-5

*This book is the accumulation of the learning of a lifetime.
It is therefore dedicated to those people who helped make me
what I am today. This includes a warm and loving family beginning
with my mother Florence Marcello Payack, who taught me the love of
the written word, my father Peter P. Payack, "The Iron Man" who
taught me the value of steadfast love. My sister Bonnie, with an
unbounded intellect, her husband Harry, a friend and advisor for
many years, their children Rachel and Alex, my sister Chrissy, with an
unbounded heart, and, of course my twin brother, Peter, the poet
laureate of Cambridge, Massachusetts, who taught me more than he'll
ever know, his wife Monica and their two sons, Michael and Peter
Paul. Then we have my two wonderful and beautiful daughters,
Elisabeth, who holds within herself a flame "of love and light and life,"
her husband Michael and son Dorian who are my technical advisors,
and Isaiah, new to the world but loving every moment of it, and my
daughter Rebecca Ashley (Bekka), a fine young woman, a fellow alum,
who is also creative director for the Global Language Monitor. Finally,
there is my loving wife Millie L. Payack, who has stood by me since the
early metafiction days, reading every word I've ever written, together
moving about the country on what has turned out to be a grand (and
continuing) adventure, cleaving together, holding the family ever
together and always tightly with her love.*

Contents

Acknowledgments

This book is the result of the hard work of many people. First, I would like to thank the Zachary Shuster Harmsworth Agency, Lane Zachary and my agent, Rachel Sussman, who guided me in this project over many months, strengthening my original vision along the way. I'd also like to acknowledge Richard Ember, my editor at Kensington Books, who was most understanding as the deadlines shifted ever so gently but, more importantly, helped shape this book, providing valuable insights, notes and suggestions throughout the process of creation and revision. I am also grateful to Michaela Hamilton, the editor-in-chief for Citadel Press, who has been a strong proponent of this book from the very beginning. Design and production of the book took dedicated efforts by Elleanore Waka, production manager, and Arthur Maisel, production editor. Included in the editorial process was the very fine work of Erin Curler, and John Dolan, with his constant advice and analysis of my early work, should be noted. I would be remiss if I did not mention the constant prayers and encouragement of my dear friend Ron Pinkston. I am deeply indebted to Robert L. Beard, a.k.a. Dr. Goodword. I would also like to thank the Global Language Monitor's Language Police, who are each expert in their individual fields, including Lou Lorenzo, Joe and Michael Marcello, Peter, Michael and Peter Paul Payack, Michael Manewitz, and Rico Blazer, among the many others who come to the Global Language Monitor website and offer their observations, criticism, and encouragement. I have very special thanks to my daughter. Elisabeth Lauren, who provided countless hours of research and editorial assistance. Finally, I'd like to thank the Lord, who provided me with the talent, native intelligence and resources to accomplish this work.

Introduction

I'll admit it: I am a language geek. Or worse.

By the time I was eight or ten years old, I was devouring every book containing "fascinating facts" I could get my hands on. I would memorize random information and then entertain (some might say terrorize) my family and friends with it. Not only would I ask them how tall Mount Everest was, I would want them to compare the current measurement with earlier estimates! (Actual height of Mount Everest: 29,028 feet. Previous recorded height: 29,000 feet. "Official" height for many years: 29,002 feet, a number chosen because it sounded more "real" than the actual, round number.) Measuring the mountain in meters (8839.81), of course, would have avoided the entire problem.

Once I reached high school, I became even more obsessed with this sort of information, and I spent my time thinking about such things as: What would happen if you emptied out "bottomless" Lake Tahoe? (The entire state of California would be covered with 14 inches of water.) Or pondering facts like: A typical human brain has about 10 billion neurons, and each neuron can theoretically be connected to every other neuron. (Meaning that there are more potential interconnections in the human brain than there are elementary particles in the universe. Which explains a lot.)

While in college, I discovered that Olympus Mons on the planet Mars is actually far taller than Mount Everest, towering some 88,585 feet (27,000.71 meters) over the Martian surface. I wrote to the editors of the *Guinness Book of Records*, explaining that this mountain should be listed as the "Tallest Mountain in the World." If, that is, you accept the definition of "the world" as "the sphere of human existence." Guinness listed it in the next edition, but labeled it the "tallest mountain in the solar system." Pshaw! (An exclamation used to express shock, contempt and disbelief.)

As I approached twenty, my mania for facts gradually evolved into a passion for words. Words, after all, were where the facts were hidden. I looked for the most interesting etymologies (*etymology*, from the French, *etymologie*; from the Latin *etymologia*; from the Greek, *etymologia*, "the true account and analysis of a word"; from *etymos*, "the true literal sense of a word," and *logos*, description; from *legein*, Greek, "to speak") I could find. I had always compared data from various sources: as a "tween" (a relatively new word in the English language), it was the *World Almanac* vs. the *Information Please Almanac* vs. the *Columbia–Viking Desk Encyclopedia*, and the like. Now it was *The Oxford English Dictionary*, Compact Edition, unabridged (with requisite magnifying glass) vs. *The Oxford English Dictionary of Etymology* vs. *Webster's New Twentieth Century Dictionary* vs. *American Heritage Dictionary*. I pored over them all, looking for discrepancies. No word was safe.

I also embarked on what many would consider a rather peculiar quest: to learn the etymology—not, mind you, the definition, but the *etymology*—of every word I encountered in my reading. I began looking up each word I couldn't already trace back to its roots, and I continued this project until I stopped coming across words whose origins were unfamiliar to me. It took about ten years. Once I got to Harvard, where I was studying comparative literature and dead languages, I decided I would also read the entire *Encyclopedia Britannica*. I wowed my friends with superfluous (but always fascinating) information: "I'm finishing up the letter *K*. Today's the day to ask me anything you need to know about anything that begins with the letter *K*!" (Oh, the state of learning in that dark age before the Internet!)

After college, I took a short detour into academic administration for a small college in Boston's Back Bay. Then I moved into the high-tech world, at a time when there were only 180 "nodes" in the world. (Nodes: points where computers can connect to one another. Today there are over 2 billion nodes. In the high-tech jargon of the '80s and '90s I would have qualified as a "dinosaur"; today I qualify as "primeval slime" or "primordial ooze." Your choice.

Given my lifelong passion for words, I finally decided—after stints as a senior executive at three Fortune 500 companies and half a dozen Silicon Valley start-ups, spin-outs, and spun-downs— to turn my avocation into a vocation. In 1999, I launched yourDictionary.com (YDC) with Dr. Robert L. Beard of Bucknell University; YDC has since grown into one of the largest language destination sites on the planet, with more than 10 million page views a month. (We bought the rights to YDC's immediate predecessor, a Web of On-line Dictionaries, the first major multilingual dictionary site on the Web—way back in 1994.) In 2003, I went one step further and established the Global Language Monitor (GLM), which systematically tracks, analyzes, and documents trends in the English language from all corners of the globe. I devised a proprietary algorithm, the Predictive Quantities Indicator (PQI), for the analysis of words and phrases in the global print media, on the Internet, and throughout the blogosphere.

At GLM, we began to look at English as *Global English*. Rather than focusing on geography (British English, American English, Caribbean English) or the psychogeography of the mind (Victorian

English in the late nineteenth century), we focused on usage—*how* English is spoken, by worldwide youth (Global YouthSpeak), by corporations, by the entertainment world, and the like. With the help of an international assemblage of professors, professional word-smiths, and bibliophiles—our language police—GLM has been documenting the latest developments in the evolution of the English language for the past five years. The results of our collective efforts have been astounding, and many in international print and elec-tronic media (such as CNN, *The New York Times*, the BBC, and PBS) and in the world of academia (at USC's Annenberg Centers for Communication and Public Diplomacy, Columbia University, the California Institute of Technology, and many other universities and institutions throughout the world) now rely on GLM for our expert analysis on language trends and their impact on politics, cul-ture, and business. We've even supplied Answers (their unique form of Questions) to *Jeopardy*, the classic television show.

We've also come to realize that there are several momentous trends that are occurring in the English language of today: (1) A vocabulary explosion: the number of everyday words we use to communicate—those recorded in dictionaries, in newspapers, in blogs and on the Internet, in correspondence to our loved ones, in classroom assignments, in paying our bills, and in recording our history—is expanding at an unprecedented rate, the total approx-imating 1 million at this very moment; and (2) A geographic ex-plosion: the English language, which at the time of Shakespeare was spoken in a narrow band in the south of Britain by only a few million people, has suddenly, and rather unexpectedly, become the language of global discourse, commerce, science, entertain-ment, and communications, with approximately 1.35 billion speakers.

As a lifelong lover of the English language, I could not be more pleased by this. And I'm thrilled to be a continuing witness to its evolution, watching and anticipating the countless new ways it will impact the lives of billions around the globe for decades (and even centuries) to come.

In the pages that follow, I will take you on a unique journey through the English language, showing how English is adding words and spreading across the globe as has no other language before it.

I will present to you many of the areas that are contributing new words and phrases to the tapestry of Global English, and I will highlight the latest developments in the language, defining new words and explaining when and why they rose to popularity. Some of the words and phrases you will see in the chapters to come will be familiar to you—these are well-known phrases whose popularity skyrocketed after being associated with unprecedented tragedy (the South Asian tsunami), spoken by a notable figure (Bushisms), or even uttered by a star on the silver or small screen (wardrobe malfunction). Other words and phrases I've highlighted are entirely new words, neologisms, coined by corporations (Google), artistic communities (hip-hop), or even ordinary men and women like you and me.

To provide you with a more complete understanding of Global English, I will compare English to the other major languages, and share with you many of the fascinating and unique facts about this language that I've gathered through my lifetime, as well as my favorite—and most surprising—word origins.

I hope to convince readers that English is growing at a phenomenal pace (one million words and counting) and, that the newest words in the English language are coming from a variety of relatively new sources (the "lishes," high technology, YouthSpeak, entertainment, and the like). Finally, I will speculate upon the future of Global English, some hundreds of years hence.

CHAPTER ONE

The Million-Word March

Never before in the history of the planet has a single language held as dominant a position as English does today. Some 1,350,000,000 people can now read this sentence in its original language. Think about that for a minute.

This fact stuns the experts, who for the last couple of decades predicted that English would be overtaken by Spanish or Chinese or some postmodern artificial language that you and I could never quite fathom, let alone speak. English was, after all, the tongue of the now-defunct British Empire, the vehicle for spreading American imperialism, and the progenitor of most of the ills of the modern world.

But a funny thing happened on the way to the funeral of the English language. It exploded! Rather than the great mass of humanity learning Chinese, the Chinese are learning English—some 250,000,000 of them by the latest count. Rather than the billion Indians of the Subcontinent rebelling against the language of their former subjugators, they are embracing it as the international language of science, engineering, and commerce. English is the primary language on the Internet, and in the entertainment world. On this planet of nearly 7,000 living languages (6,920 to be precise), English has become the first truly global language, the world's lingua franca.

What does this all mean?

It means that the long anticipated arrival of the "global village" will now be recorded in English. It may take a village to raise a child, but it will also take at least a few English speakers to be present to communicate with the other global villages or, at the very least, to install the electronic infrastructure, the Internet, the landlines, and the VCRs, DVDs, and Xboxes the villagers will demand. It assures English a preeminent role in the world of languages for generations to come. No other language comes close in the extent of either its vocabulary or its geographic reach. And with this incredible number of words from which to choose, English is well positioned to continue as the leading language for arts and letters, for technology and commerce. Over a billion English speakers, artists, engineers,

> ► Nontechnical English has over 1,000,000 words.
>
> ► Spanish has more than 250,000 words.
>
> ► German has about 185,000 words.
>
> ► French has fewer than 100,000 words.
>
> ► Chinese has about 50,000 ideograms, each glyph representing as many as eight words.
>
> ► The Bible contains fewer than 20,000 different words. (Actually, 12,143 in the English, 783,137 total in the King James Version, 8,674 in the Hebrew Old Testament, and 5,624 in the Greek New Testament.)
>
> ► 24,000 differing words are to be found in the complete works of Shakespeare. He invented about 1,700 of them.

scientists, and CEOs who want to directly reach the broadest possible audience now have the tool to do so: the English language.

Writers of English have the good fortune of having hundreds of thousands of words from which to choose. English supplies at least three words for any idea; each rooted in the Latin, the Germanic or Saxon tongues, and the Greek. Think of a word for human habitation: city, town, metropolis, and so on. And that's just the start. In the English-speaking world, we also owe a heavy debt to Algonquian, and Hebrew, and Malay (ketchup, anyone?), and Maori, and Zulu, and Hmong, among a multitude of others. You can probably spot the beginnings of a trend here.

And then there is the entire realm of "jargon," scientific and otherwise, the specialized patois or vocabularies known only to those in specific fields. Computer-related jargon is multiplying at an extraordinary rate. And since English has become the common language of the Internet, English words are being created and non-English words co-opted at an ever-quickening pace.

Which brings us to the number of words in English.

The Global Language Monitor's English Language WordClock has attempted to pinpoint the precise number of words in the English language at a given point in time. To do so, we first established a base number of words in the language using the generally accepted unabridged dictionaries (the O.E.D., Merriam-Webster's,* Macquarie's, etc.), containing the historic core of the English lan-

---

* Note on the Million-Word March: The Global Language Monitor's estimate of the number of words in the English language takes a relatively conservative approach. For example, it should be noted that the introduction to Merriam-Webster's 3rd International claims about 450,000 words are listed in that dictionary. The introduction goes on to state, "the number of words available is always far in excess of and for a single volume dictionary many times the number that can possibly be included." Many times the 450,000 included words of course results in a number far in excess of 1,000,000.

The worldwide media have, indeed, shown intense interest in this linguistic milestone. The *Washington Post*, numerous U.S. and Australian media outlets, two BBC radio stations, and a number of London newspapers have already run contests to nominate the millionth word. (The contributions include *percycution*: giving your child a name he will hate for the rest of his life; *martyration*: a request for only thirty-six virgins in paradise; and *enamortization*: to fall rashly in love with an object or person, and end up paying for it for the next twenty years.) And as a wonderful surprise to those of us who work at GLM, school children in both the United Kingdom and the United States have been sending us their millionth word suggestions.

guage: every word found in the works of Shakespeare, the King James Bible, Chaucer, and the other classics.

As we used our proprietary algorithm, the Predictive Quantities Indicator, to track the frequency of English words and phrases, GLM also assigned a number to the rate of creation of new words and the adoption and absorption of foreign vocabulary into the language. Our result, although an estimate, has been quite useful as a starting point of discussion for laypersons, students, and scholars the world over.

And one thing we know for certain is that the expansion of the language is speeding up every day. The Global Language Monitor now stands poised to announce the introduction of the one-millionth word into the English language. With the present word count standing around 995,000 words, we estimate that the Global Codex of Expository English should have reached the 1,000,000th word mark by the time you read these words.

This all being said, I now unequivocally state that as of 1:16 P.M. (Pacific) on the 20th day of January in the year 2008 AD (or CE,

How the PQI Works

Originally created as the Political-Sensitivity Quotient Index, the PQI is a proprietary algorithm (a series of equations) that tracks the frequency of words and phrases in global print media, on the Internet, throughout the blogosphere, and in proprietary databases such as Factiva and Lexis-Nexis. The original idea was to objectively analyze political "hot buttons" or buzzwords for what they really are: words of profound impact that often skew the actual message and can short-circuit the process of analysis and debate. The effect is multiplied many times over once these buzzwords are launched into the ether through the ever-increasing number (and variety) of media outlets.

The PQI searches for the following:

➤ *Keywords:* Words that serve as reference points

➤ *Phrases:* Series of words that serve as reference points to the keywords

➤ *Excluders:* Words or phrases that must be excluded from the PQI analysis

➤ *Penumbra Words:* Words or series of words that frequently surround the keywords, phrases, and excluders

There are actually two differing PQIs. When analyzing words and phrases in political contexts, GLM uses the Political-Sensitivity Quotient Index; when analyzing words and phrases in any other context, GLM uses a slightly different Predictive Quantities Indicator.

The algorithms, themselves, can be used to analyze any number of language usage problems or situations. This is because the PQI seems to reduce complexity, or even chaos, into easily understandable metrics. This being so, the larger (and more chaotic) the Internet becomes, the more powerful the results of the PQI should be.

(continued)

The PQI is a surprisingly powerful analytical tool in the real world. An example: the 2004 U.S. presidential election. The controversy surrounding the exit polls, which did not appear to mirror the will of the electorate, astonished many political analysts. But GLM had been tracking the electorate for nine months, and we had picked up on a trend: the electorate was looking at all the issues through the lens of "moral values," viewing thirteen of the top twenty issues tracked in the PQI as a series of moral quandaries. To them, the Iraq War was a moral issue, outsourcing American jobs was a moral issue, tax breaks or relief were moral issues, and so on. We released our results the day before the election. But it wasn't until the media uproar over the exit polls that the impact of PQI's findings became widely understood.

whatever your preference), there were approximately 995,116 words in the English language, plus or minus a handful.

Choose well among them.

If Global English Is Growing, Is It Alive?

Yes, it fulfills most criteria for life.

It grows, expands, sheds words, leaps over physical, geographic, and political boundaries, and persists for generations (or even millennia). Language also has the seeming ability to morph at will, to resist any attempt to control or guide its direction or growth.

For example, L'Académie française was created in 1635 under the watchful eye of Cardinal Richelieu. According to Article 24 of the academy's charter, "the primary function of the Académie will be to work, with all possible care and diligence, to give our language definite rules and to make it pure, eloquent, and capable of dealing with art and science." Over the years this task has become significantly more difficult, as the language wants to ingest new words and will simply not follow such dictates. Recent attempts by the French academy to restrict words such as hamburger, iPod, and e-mail have produced controversial (and sometimes comical) attempts to keep the English language at bay.

In 2003, a French commission with loose ties to L'Académie declared the word *e-mail* to be unworthy of the French lexicon. The preferred term was one more frequently used by French-speaking Quebecois: *courriel.* This caused a huge kerfuffle (variation of *carfuffle*, from Scottish Gaelic *cearr*, "wrong, awkward," and *fuffle*, chiefly British, "to become disheveled"). Of course, the Web-savvy French youth never even noticed the dictate, and continued using the already accepted Internet lingo, *e-mail* or *email*, though, as one might expect, *courriel* has had greater acceptance among government ministries and the like. Some years later, there are about 34 million Google references to various forms of the word *courriel.* But there remain some 2 *billion* references to the word *e-mail.*

In effect, language itself appears to decide which words it will accept or reject, by a process that is both difficult to discern or deconstruct.

> ► *Approximately 60 percent of the world's radio programs are in English.*
>
> ► *About 75 percent of the world's snail mail is written in English.*
>
> ► *About 90 percent the world's e-mails are written in English.*

Why Are There Objections to Recognizing English as the Global Language?

Frequently, I am asked by academics, some angry, why I think the English language is so special. My answer is simple: I do not think Global English is special. I am simply reporting a rather interesting set of converging facts that are, indeed, special (*special,* "surpassing what is common or usual; exceptional").

The fact that a single language has undergone this dramatic growth throughout its history, and now dominates the worlds of commerce, technology, science, communications, and cyberspace, is most definitely special.

The fact that for the first time in world history a language is truly global, that is spanning the entire globe (and not just Europe, as in the case of Medieval Latin, or Greek in the lands of Alexander's conquests), is unequivocally special. In light of facts like these, how can anyone deny that the expansion of Global English is a true phenomenon?

In the early 2000s, the member nations of the UN were asked which language should be the dominant one in official communications between and among embassies. More than 120 chose English. Some 40 selected French, and 20 selected Spanish.

The main argument against Global English is that the rise of English is due primarily to cultural hegemony. That the cultural-industrial complex of Western civilization, and of the United States in particular, is responsible for spreading English to all corners of the globe. True? True enough. Has this ever happened before, to this extent, in global history? Most definitely not.

Did anyone listening to rap music in the South Bronx in the 1970s even imagine that hip-hop would emerge a generation hence in Rio, Warsaw, Bangladesh, Dakar, Mexico City, Lima, Moscow,

---

Uranus, the seventh planet (named after the Greek god of the sky), has a number of satellites. Did you know they are each named for characters found in the works of Shakespeare and Alexander Pope?

- Cordelia (*King Lear*)
- Ophelia (*Hamlet*)
- Bianca (*Taming of the Shrew*)
- Cressida (*Troilus and Cressida*)
- Desdemona (*Othello*)
- Juliet (*Romeo and Juliet*)
- Portia (*Merchant of Venice*)
- Rosalind (*As You Like It*)
- Belinda (Pope's *Rape of the Lock*)
- Puck (*A Midsummer Night's Dream*)
- Miranda (*The Tempest*)
- Ariel (*The Tempest*)
- Umbriel (Pope's *Rape of the Lock*)
- Titania (*A Midsummer Night's Dream*)
- Oberon (*A Midsummer Night's Dream*)
- Caliban (*The Tempest*)
- Sycorax (*The Tempest*)
- Prospero (*The Tempest*)
- Setebos (*The Tempest*)
- Stephano (*The Tempest*)
- Trinculo (*The Tempest*)

Ho Chi Minh City, Sydney, Winnipeg, and Katmandu? Maybe, if they had followed the global migration of jazz during the early part of the twentieth century. Sure, cultural hegemony fuels Global English. But it's a cultural hegemony driven by the people, and driven from the ground up.

And "cultural hegemony" is the key term here. I do not think the resistance to Global English would be nearly as intense if you could truly separate the words, the thoughts, and the actions, from the language itself. But as you will see in the following chapters, separating the cultural artifacts (or *artefacts* in Britain) from the language can be a very difficult thing to do, indeed.

Does Language Actually Shape the Way We Think?

Yes. And no. This possibility is the root of many fears about Global English hegemony. If more and more people speak American English, will more and more people act, think, and feel like Americans?

In linguistics, this fear goes back to the Sapir-Whorf hypothesis, which states that there is a relationship between the "grammatical categories" of the language (or languages) you speak, and the way you see your world. It suggests that the particular nature of a language profoundly influences the thought of its speakers, with different language patterns producing different results, different thoughts.

So, does language actually shape the way you think? Yes. But can you use a language to shape the way you want *others* to think? Only in the most cursory manner. Case in point: the old Soviet Bloc. When the Berlin Wall finally came down and people just streamed across the old East–West border, there were numerous interviews with the East Germans. Many were asked why they were leaving the security of their homes for the uncertainty of the West. Among the top answers were: bananas (which were in perpetually short supply) and Levi's (which had to be smuggled in). Decades of having their words shaped and measured by the old Soviet propaganda machine had met their match in Western advertising. In the government's battle to keep Western words—and, by extension, Western ideas—away from the populace, the words prevailed.

In the final analysis, it is the language itself that accepts or rejects your final recommendations.

What Is a Word?

What is a word? This, of course, may seem a rather basic question. After all, this book is full of tens of thousands of the little critters, each page crawling (and nearly overflowing) with hundreds of 'em. But really: What makes a word a word?

"A thing spoken; something that is said," according to Webster's. Note that the definition is not:

> - A string of letters
> - A string of letters separated by spaces
> - Things found upon a page

Etymology: Middle English, from Old English; akin to Old High German *wort*, "word"; Latin *verbum*, Greek *eirein*, "to say, speak"; Hittite *weriya-*, "to call, name."

My preferred definition: "A thought spoken."

Where Do New Words Come From?

New words evidently bubble up to the surface of our minds, pass from our minds through our mouths, and are launched into the ether. Like everything else, they are subject to the forces of natural selection: Some make it, some don't. Some words make it for reasons that are evident even to the novice word hunter, whereas others inexplicably persevere, confounding even the most experienced of etymologists.

Most new words (or new uses of old words) come from these sources:

> *Science/Technology:* The necessity to find a name for a new process, substance, organism, or thing leads to a new word in the lexicon. Internet-related words are good examples: Internet, Intranet, Unix, Linux, CoBol, C++, bandwidth, software, hardware, freeware, vaporware, etc.

> *Onomatopoeia:* Onomatopoeia, "barking words," are words that sound like the sounds they represent. A perfect example is *Arrgh!* that was recently repopularized by the *Pirates of the Caribbean* movie franchise.

Little-Known Fact About the Name "Pluto"

Pluto is named after American astronomer Percival Lowell (1855–1916), who was fascinated by what he called Planet X, the supposed ninth planet of the solar system. His theory was based on small perturbations in the orbits of Neptune and Uranus, then the most distant planets. Eight years after Lowell's death, Pluto was discovered by Clyde Tombaugh, who used Percival Lowell's initials as the first two letters of the planet's name. It also maintained the tradition of naming planets after Greek and Roman gods, since Pluto is the Roman god of the underworld. (The earth remains the only exception being named after the most common substance of its topography—earth.)

- *Brand Names:* Every year, there are about 100,000 new consumer packaged goods introduced in America and another 100,000 introduced worldwide. Some of these names enter our vocabulary. Think Xbox and iPod.

- *Domain Names:* There are approximately 75 million domain names, and some of them seep into the language, like MySpace and YouTube.

Who Decides When a Word Becomes Part of the Language?

You do. Dictionaries, for the most part, are *descriptive* in nature rather than *prescriptive.* This means that once a word has reached a certain level of usage, it's included in the dictionaries. It also means that the dictionary you use does not tell you *how* to pronounce a word. Rather, it lists the pronunciations actually used by English speakers, in the order of their prevalence (if there is more than one pronunciation). When a pronunciation is localized to a specific region, say, New England or the English Midlands, the regional pronunciation is listed as such. If a city name has several possible pronunciations, the local pronunciation is listed first. After all, it is *their* city.

Case in point: New Orleans. You can pronounce it three (or more) ways: nōō ôr′ lē- ənz, nōō ôr′ lənz, or nô′ lənz. And all these pronunciations would be considered acceptable, although the one you choose does tag you for your upbringing, your socio-economic background, or the like. Another case in point: Noo Yawk.

I learned all of this when I was a student in the early '70s. One lovely New England morning, my wife, Millie, and I had decided to drive the 90 miles out to Springfield, Massachusetts—home of the G. C. Merriam printing company, the makers of Webster's—to see how a dictionary was made. We arrived unannounced; the editor in chief, Frederick C. Mish, came out of his office to personally greet us. He was so surprised that we had driven all the way from Cambridge that he repeated several times that "no jobs were currently available." Of course, we weren't looking for employment. We were looking to learn about dictionaries!

Finally we convinced him that we weren't job-hunting, and he agreed to take us on a tour. He guided us through the rather small offices, where we saw the researchers poring over their dockets, reading magazines and newspapers, circling words of interest and clipping them out along with the context of their usage. I was fascinated.

Eventually we got around to discussing the issue of differing pronunciations. I proudly announced that if a modern word was based upon one of the Greek or Latin classics, and its proper pronunciations was in dispute, then it should be pronounced according to the ways of the ancients. I used, as an example, the word *quasi*:

> PRONUNCIATION: kwzā-si, -s, kwäz'ē
>
> ADJECTIVE: Having a likeness to something; resembling: a quasi success.
>
> ETYMOLOGY: Middle English, "as if," from Old French, from Latin *quasi, quam,* "as" (*American Heritage*)

I insisted the second pronunciation was the more appropriate one, since it was closer to the original Latin. I, of course, had fallen directly into the (slightly elitist) prescriptive trap. I was gently reprimanded by the editor in chief, who explained to me that dictionaries are not about what *should be*, but rather are about what *is*.

It was at that moment I discovered that I had a lot more to learn about dictionaries.

What Is Webster's?

Noah Webster compiled the first dictionary of the "American" language in 1828, which he first titled *A Compendious Dictionary of the English Language*, and then wisely retitled *An American Dictionary of the English Language* (1828). It contained some 70,000 entries, newly standardized spellings (such as *wimmen*, which never caught on except in Popeye cartoons), and an extra two letters for the alphabet (he kept both the letters *i* and *j*, which for hundreds of years had been used interchangeably, and the letters *u* and *uu*—a.k.a. *w*—which led to much confusion in spelling).

Webster believed that a new nation born in revolution should extend the revolution into every aspect of society. One of these beliefs was that standardization of spelling would make words more accessible to everyone. So in the evolution of the English language, his *Compendious Dictionary* was more important as a *speller* than as a *definer* of words.

What Webster did not do, however, was protect his name, and over time it became synonymous with "dictionary." Which is why we have a plethora of Webster's-branded dictionaries (Merriam-Webster's, Webster's New World, Webster's 20th Century, etc.), some of great authority but others of little.

The influence of Benjamin Franklin upon Noah Webster is often overlooked, as is Franklin's work on Simplified English Spelling, *A Scheme for a new Alphabet and a Reformed Mode of Spelling*, in which he used six invented letters to replace the letters *c, j, q, w, x,* and *y*. Franklin's idea was to assign a single sound to each letter. He passed on his theory and leaden type fonts to the much younger Webster.

Webster has become a brand name, and because of overwhelming acceptance in the marketplace it has slipped into the public domain and no longer enjoys any legal protection as intellectual property. In this way, Webster's is the equivalent of Kleenex and Xerox, branded properties that have also moved into the public domain as being synonymous with "tissue" and "copy" or "copy machine," respectively. Moving in that direction today are both Google and iPod.

Appropriately, the Indo-European root etymology for *webh-* means "to weave" with derivatives that include *web*, *weevil*, and *wobble*.

And a dictionary is certainly a book compiled or woven together into a meaningful whole.

What Are the Parts of a Word?

At first, this may seem like a simple question: We all know that words are composed of letters, and, beyond that, vowels, consonants, and syllables. But as any linguist will tell you, the reality of word composition is much more complex. It's almost like the subatomic world, which is awash in ever smaller exotic particles (quarks, bosons, leptons, etc.), which we know are there but never actually perceive. That's what's going in the linguistic world. For example, it's common knowledge that there are a limited number of vowels in the English language (*a, e, i, o, u*, and sometimes *y* or *w*). But in the chart on the next page you can see the vowels encountered in the English alphabet, according to the International Phonetic Alphabet (or IPA).

IPA SYMBOL	EXAMPLE
iː	three
I	bin
æ	fat
ɑː	far
ɔː	sort
ʊ	put
uː	boot
ʌ	up
ɜː	her
ə	until
e	bed
ɒ	rock

Source: www.usingenglish.com/handouts/beginner/phonemic-script.pdf.

The first thing you might notice is that there are actually *twelve* vowels represented, as opposed to the *five* you were taught in school. (Just as you once thought that an atom only consisted of neutrons, protons and electrons.) This is because each vowel listed above represents a different sound, or *morpheme*. A morpheme is the smallest *meaningful* linguistic unit. Morphemes are composed of *phonemes*, which are the tiniest units of sound that can make a difference in meaning, such as the "h" in hat and the "c" in cat from one another. In other words, linguists classify vowels not merely as letters, but as sounds.

Many morphemes cannot stand as words on their own. A morpheme is *free* if it can stand alone, or *bound* if it is used exclusively alongside a free morpheme. Because the tone of a morpheme may actually change its meaning, morphemes can be understood only in context.

A famous example is the word *dogs*.

Get ready for this one: *Dogs* is composed of two morphemes and one syllable. OK, so you knew about the single syllable, but perhaps you didn't know that the letter *s*, the "plural marker" for English nouns, is its own morpheme. Ah! So the same goes for the word *nouns*: one syllable and two morphemes. And because we can distinguish the sound of the *s* at the end of the word, we know that it's also a phoneme. So now you can see that *s* can be both a phoneme and morpheme. And neither phoneme nor morpheme need be syllables.

Believe it or not, things get even more complicated.

> ▸ According to SIL International, the relationship between a morpheme and its morphs and allomorphs is parallel to the relationship between a phoneme and its phones and allophones. (Huh?)

> ▸ A morpheme is manifested as one or more *morphs* (surface forms) in different environments. These morphs are called *allomorphs*. (Say what?)

> ▸ A phoneme is manifested as one or more *phones* (phonetic sounds) in different environments. These phones are called *allophones*. (I was at a student council meeting the afternoon they taught that in high school.)

Source: SIL.org.

I'm revealing this esoteric knowledge to you so you can understand that language is far more complicated than even a student, writer, or voracious reader might ever imagine. You might be asking: What does all this mean to Global English?

It means that words, even very tiny, very familiar ones, are a lot more complicated than most people think.

It means that the philosophical constructs behind language are deeper and more complex than most of us realize.

It means that fierce academic battles are being fought over words that make those of Middle Earth seem like child's play. And, for everyone that believes in the existence of a new word, someone else will dispute it.

Where Did English Come From?

If we trace it way, way back, as far as we can go, we learn that the English language began with the Proto-Indo-Europeans. Sounds made up, doesn't it? But it's not: The Proto-Indo-Europeans were the speakers of a prehistoric tongue of the Chalcolithic and early Bronze Age that was the ancestor of the Indo-European language and, hence, English.

We know very little about these people. They are theorized to have lived between 3000–4000 BC. They lived in the Eurasian steppe, cultivated cattle and horses, had solid wheels, and practiced agriculture and hunting. They were a patrilineal society and were partially nomadic. That's all we know. They left no trace, beyond the words we now speak. No monuments. No gravesites. No ruins. Not

What Is Grimm's Law?

Created by Jakob Grimm (of the famous storytellers the Brothers Grimm) in 1822, Grimm's law noted the shift from Proto-Indo-European sounds to Proto-Germanic sounds. For example, the sound *p* (such as in *pes*, Latin, "foot") morphed into *f* (as in, Swedish, *fot*, "foot").

a single inscription, not a single bone. Incredible as it may now seem, their legacy has passed down through the centuries because of their language, which formed the basis for 40 percent of the world's languages, including English.

Some 40 percent perhaps as many as 50 percent of people now walking upon this planet (a planet that has no official name, by the way—but that's another topic for another book) speak some derivation of Proto-Indo-European.

Here are some of the language families currently spoken that descend from that ancient tongue:

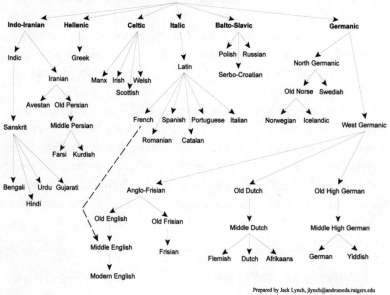

Prepared by Jack Lynch, jlynch@andromeda.rutgers.edu

Did you notice which European languages are not *listed, because they do* not *descend from Proto-Indo-European? Basque, Finnish, and Hungarian, to name but three.*

If English Is a Lingua Franca, Isn't That a Form of Cultural Hegemony?

English as a lingua franca is different from English as a second language. We are all well aware of how successfully English has served as the common means of discourse in any number of global contexts, from business to education to high technology to entertainment. This does not necessarily mean that English must also become a cultural franca as well.

If you take the view of language as a living entity, there is even less concern about American/British ownership (for instance, the roots of hip hop aren't traced to New York, LA, or London, but to the back streets of Kingston, Jamaica). This living English language will undoubtedly continue to incorporate various standards, accents, and usages as it evolves through the next millennium. Recent studies have shown that students around the world do not think of English as the property of America, the UK, the Commonwealth, or of anyone else for that matter. In their view, they are the owners of the language.

And since Global English means different things to different peoples, societies, and cultures, perhaps it might be viewed as a global commodity best implemented locally in the "think globally, act locally" construct. To recall Chairman Mao, we appear to be witnessing the blooming of a 1,000 English-language flowers as it takes root from Shanghai to Chennai, from La Paz to Ho Chi Minh City.

In the global marketplace, if you follow what is happening with English as the corporate lingua franca, it becomes obvious that corporate affairs are being handled by people from a host of national, cultural, and linguistic backgrounds to a degree once unimagined and unimaginable. Rather than stratifying global relations under Western domination, English is enabling the world to communicate and connect in partnership through a common language—a true lingua franca.

What Is the Future of the English Language?

The last time a language was a serious contender for "universal" or "global" status was in the High Middle Ages, when Latin could be heard from the British Isles to Constantinople, Alexandria, and beyond. Latin was the lingua franca for more than a thousand years. Of course, the geographic extent of Latin's footprint was, perhaps, less than 20 percent of the then-known world.

Latin is now the official language only of Vatican City.

There are a number of possible scenarios for the future of Global English that we will discuss in the final chapter. However, two are worth noting here:

1. Under the weight of billions of speakers, it collapses into its various "lishes" (Chinglish, Hinglish, Spanglish, etc.). Eventually, these lishes branch so far from standard English that they become mutually unintelligible tongues sharing a common root.

2. An internationally standardized form of English facilitates global communication in ways yet unseen.

It probably won't surprise you that I favor the second scenario.

Chances are, we can rest assured that, for now anyway, Global English will continue to dominate. Yet although a mind-boggling percentage of human beings alive today speak this common tongue, only the rare person has given much thought to the words we use day in and day out.

CHAPTER TWO

From the Corner of Hollywood and Vine

How Movies and Television Help Shape Global Culture

"HollyWords" are words or phrases imported from Hollywood that have an undeniable impact upon the language. Some are direct quotations from film that capture the national zeitgeist, while others emerge from our celebrity-obsessed chatter. All are tied to a cultural moment and testify to Hollywood's power to change the way we communicate.

Why do we care?

The author Jorge Luis Borges maintained that the popularity of the western genre of movies was due to the way they played out mythic roles for us, those of the Greek, Roman, and Northern gods. Just like Zeus or Jupiter, John Wayne, Clint Eastwood, and others seemed to have the superhuman ability to punish wrongdoers and ensure that order was maintained. The "spaghetti" western typifies the genre: A "man with no name" rides into town, speaks spare words, lays low the bad guys, and then continues on his journey. If some problem or obstacle looms larger than the protagonist can handle on his own, a deus ex machina (an unexpected event introduced to resolve a situation) descends from the sky (or the barn hayloft) to the rescue. These films all play out on an epic scale, amid the sweeping vistas of sky and earth at its most elemental.

And so it is with the rest of what appears on the silver screen. Movies tell their stories according to dream logic, where the juxtaposition of images is the logic itself, which need not be drawn out in words, or even actions. Whatever the genre—whether it be a spaghetti western or an action adventure or a romantic comedy—a film's unique combination of images and words can often impact our culture, and, by extension, our vocabularies.

When particular sets of words that are spoken in a movie stir the spirit, or make us spring out of our seats, or leave us feeling particularly repulsed, they should at least be noted if not necessarily honored. It is in this spirit that these words have been compiled from the films of recent years. The annual Oscar ceremony is an appropriate time to measure the state of Global English, because it's all on view: the soaring prose, the refinement, and the vulgarity.

TOP HOLLYWORDS OF RECENT YEARS

"ARRGH!" (*Pirates of the Caribbean: Dead Man's Chest*): An onomatopoeic term that is spreading ever more deeply into popular culture.

BROKEBACK: From the Oscar-winning 2005 film *Brokeback Mountain*. A cultural phenomenon with over 30 million references online. Most common meanings include "gay," "effeminate," or "living a secret gay life" (as in *brokeback marriage*). The word now has its own Chinese ideogram and is a prime candidate for the next edition of the *Contemporary Chinese Dictionary*.

"CHICA CHICA, BOOM BOOM" (*Happy Feet*): Just one sign that an attack of spontaneous dancing is about to begin.

CLASSIC FIGURES (*Dreamgirls*): The curvier dimensions of women that, for more than 200,000 years of human history, were the celebrated forms. Coincidentally, anorexia and bulimia did not arise until the mid-twentieth century.

DAME (*Notes on a Scandal*): Dame Judi Dench. What more can be said?

"THE DETAILS OF YOUR INCOMPETENCE DO NOT INTEREST ME." (*The Devil Wears Prada*): Meryl Streep's not-so-nurturing remark to those who surround (and serve) her.

"DON'T PANIC": From the *Hitchhiker's Guide to the Galaxy*. Excellent advice for just about any situation in the twenty-first century.

FILM NOIR (*The Black Dahlia*): A category of film that hearkens back to the classics of the 1940s and '50s (and a movie that makes us miss them).

GIGLI: From the movie of the same name starring Ben Affleck and Jennifer Lopez, considered by many to be one of the worst films ever made by a major studio (along with *Ishtar* and *Waterworld*). "Gigli" became a new way to express extreme disappointment, as in "that was gigli, gigli bad."

HAND WASHING: Behavior shown by Howard Hughes in *The Aviator*, Pontius Pilate in *The Passion*, and the world community in *Hotel Rwanda*.

"HELP!—¡Ayúdenme!—HELP!" (*Babel*): A cry for help in a land apparently without ears.

HERO (*Flags of Our Fathers*): Something the heroes of

Iwo Jima never asked to be, much like their 9/11 grandsons.

"HIGH FIVE!!!! IT'S SEXY TIME!" (*Borat*): Borat's catch-phrase, typically used when he was about to do something shocking on his American tour. Now more broadly used as high-spirited banter.

LABYRINTH (*Pan's Labyrinth*): A word that, because of this powerful film, is gradually replacing *quagmire* in popularity.

"MAKE US DISAPPEAR!" (*The Illusionist*): The leading lady's request to a young magician (Ed Norton).

MAYA YUCATECO (*Apocolypto*): Mel's Gibson's choice of language for his film depicting a collapsing civilization, it's actually still spoken by some 6 million Maya descendants in the Yucatán.

A MORAL ISSUE (*An Inconvenient Truth*): Al Gore's chilling documentary, about climate change and its ultimate impact upon the human environment, explains that global warning is a moral issue, not a political one.

NAZI BULLETS (*Little Miss Sunshine*): "I still got Nazi bullets in my ass." Grandpa's excuse to do or say anything he pleases.

"NON SERVIAM" (*The Departed*): "I will not serve," from James Joyce's *A Portrait of the Artist as a Young Man* becomes Frank Costello's pledge to refuse to be a product of his environment. He wants his "environment to be a product of me."

OCD (OBSESSIVE-COMPULSIVE DISORDER): From *The Aviator*. Leonardo DiCaprio's portrayal of Howard

Hughes makes the small screen's *Monk* look like a model of mental clarity.

PARLEY: From *Pirates of the Caribbean*. The pirate's "code of the Brethren" states that, if requested, one cannot be harmed until one has had this audience with the captain.

PETRONOIA (*Syriana*): The fear that a collapse in the oil industry will precipitate a global economic crisis. Not exactly an irrational fear.

PURSUIT (*Pursuit of Happyness*): A word repopularized by the title of Will Smith's inspirational film, from a phrase originally penned by Thomas Jefferson some 230 years ago.

A RELUCTANT CANNIBAL (*Last King of Scotland*): The illiterate, brutal African dictator Idi Amin, portrayed by Forest Whitaker, who was rumored to feast upon his victims.

ROTEMORIZING (*Akeelah and the Bee*): The technique of blindly memorizing spelling words.

SMITHS: From *The Matrix* and its sequels. To lack individuality, like the multiduplicated Agent Smith.

SNAP: From the feel-good remake of *Freaky Friday*, starring Lindsay Lohan. Used as in "Oh, snap!" meaning, "very cool!"

UNDERSTATED: From *Lost in Translation*. Originally used to describe Bill Murray's elegant, understated performance, later becoming a synonym for a "sure thing" transformed into a "loser."

WHO ARE YOU WEARING? (Or, for those of you who remember your elementary school grammar classes, *Whom are you wearing?*): From the various red-carpet shows, preceding major televised award ceremonies, when inquiring about the designer of a star's wardrobe.

"WILL SOMEONE PLEASE SAVE THESE PEOPLE FROM THEMSELVES!" (*The Queen*): Tony Blair's observations of the Royals as he attempts to heal the rift between the Queen and her subjects after the death of Princess Diana.

Of course, words from the entertainment industry have been invading the English language for the better part of a century. Before the global village, before mass media, before the blogosphere, before the Internet, before cable, before television, before FM, before AM, before talkies, even before vaudeville—there was still entertainment, meaning there were still HollyWords. Probably the first HollyWord was *nickelodeon*.

TOP HOLLYWORDS AND PHRASES OF YESTERYEAR

THE A-LIST: The hypothetical list of the top rank of Hollywood actors, directors, producers, and others in the industry.

BLACKLIST: The Hollywood blacklist of suspected communist "sympathizers" first appeared in November 1947 and persisted into the '60s.

B-MOVIE: A low-budget commercial release that usually was the second half of a double feature. Not intended as an art-house film.

BONZO: A monkey made famous by future president Ronald Reagan. Or is it the other way around?

CINERAMA: VistaVision, CinemaScope, Panavision, and other innovative film formats, which were meant to combat the incursion of television.

"FRANKLY, SCARLETT, I DON'T GIVE A DAMN": One of the first profanities to grace the silver screen (from *Gone With the Wind*).

HOLLYWOOD: Originally "the Holly tract," a village a few miles up the dirt road from L.A.

THE HOLLYWOOD SIGN: Originally, the 1923 sign read HOLLYWOODLAND to advertise a new housing tract. Since then it has become the symbol of all things Hollywood.

MICKEY MOUSE: Initially named "Steamboat Willie," this mouse helped catapult Walt Disney's original creation into a global empire.

MOVIE: The audience's preferred term for "motion picture" or "film."

NICKELODEON: The prototype movie theater where millions flocked beginning in 1905 in a converted storefront in Pittsburgh, Pennsylvania. Within three years, there were eight thousand nickelodeons.

NOIR: Film noir, French for "black film," is a genre of movies popularized by such directors as Alfred Hitchcock, Billy Wilder, and Orson Welles in the 1940s and '50s. (The term was, amazingly, unknown to the creators of the genre.)

ROSEBUD: From one of the greatest movies of all time, *Citizen Kane*. At the same time, one of the weakest climaxes. All this for a sled!? How about a dog?

SILVER SCREEN: The term "silver lenticular (*lenticular*, 'of or relating to a lens') screen" referred to the silver content that provided the screen's particular brightness.

TALKIE: Movies with "synchronized sound." In one of the earliest talkies, *The Jazz Singer*, Al Jolson spoke only a few words, including, "You ain't heard nothing yet."

"A VERBAL AGREEMENT ISN'T WORTH THE PAPER IT'S WRITTEN ON": One of Sam Goldwyn's priceless aphorisms.

YESTERYEAR: A Hollywood "westernism" for "days of yore" or "times passed."

HOLLYWORD BACKGROUNDER: WORDS YOU NEED TO KNOW BEFORE YOU ARE IN THE KNOW

THE ACADEMY: Actually, AMPAS, the Academy of Motion Picture Arts and Sciences.

ANIMATION: (1) A brand-new Oscar category. (2) An actor's response to winning an Oscar (case in point, Roberto Benigni, 1999).

BIOPIC: Insider jargon for a film with biographical content.

BLOCKBUSTER: A film grossing more than $100 million in the United States and $200 million worldwide.

BOMB: A film without legs.

BO: Box office. The receipts ("take") for a film.

THE BUZZ: Positive word of mouth that causes excitement among those who have not yet seen the film.

CAMEO: Small role for a star in a movie.

CLEAVAGE: The visible portion of an actress's "golden globes," often showcased in a couture gown on the red carpet.

GAFFER: The chief lighting technician.

GRIP: The technician in charge of set production equipment, including the movement of dollies around the set.

GROSS: The total amount of money a movie makes.

HOLLYWOOD BOWL: A concert venue set in a natural amphitheater, originally called Daisey Dell.

INDIE: An independent film. Where some of the real talent and creativity in Hollywood is often quietly spotlighted.

IN THE CAN: A film or piece of a film that is all finished shooting and judged good enough to be developed and available for the next stage—editing.

KEY GRIP: The head grip in a production.

LEGS: When a film's receipts continue for a long run, often the result of "buzz."

OSCAR: Oddly named statuette. Each Oscar is $13\frac{1}{2}$ inches tall, weighs $8\frac{1}{2}$ pounds, and consists of a base metal that is sequentially covered by copper, nickel, silver, and finally finished in 24-karat gold. The name comes from past director of the Academy, Margaret Herrick, who remarked that their award statue looked like her Uncle Oscar.

THE PAVILION: As in the Dorothy Chandler Pavilion, the choice Hollywood venue of yore, since eclipsed by the Kodak Center.

PREMIERE: The debut of a film.

PRINT: A copy of a film distributed to theaters around the world. Despite numbering in the hundreds of thousands, prints of pre-1960 flicks are rare.

PRODUCER: The person who gambles a fortune on whether the director, production company, and cast will produce a product that will return more than his investment. As a rule of thumb, the larger the number of producers, the lower the quality of the film.

SAG AWARDS: Awards presented by actors themselves via the Screen Actors' Guild.

SCORE: Music accompanying a film.

SHOT LIST: The list of scenes or "shots" logged as they are filmed, to help in the editing.

SPECIAL EFFECTS, OR FX: Technical effects added to a movie to enhance reality or create unreality.

SUNDANCE: The premier festival for indies.

SUNSET STRIP: Area in Hollywood that is the erstwhile center of the industry.

TAKES: Multiple versions of the same shot.

THE INDUSTRY: The motion picture industry. Always pronounced with a lowering of the voice and always with the definite article, as in "*The* industry."

THREE-PEAT: An Oscar win three years running. This has never been done: Only five actors have won Oscars back to back, but no one has ever won them back to back to back.

TRAILER: Short pieces shown before the feature film, advertising future movies.

WRAP: The completion of shooting for the day.

TeleWords

There's no doubt that television has a profound influence on how we communicate. TeleWords are television buzzwords that emerge from game shows, sitcoms, dramas, news coverage, or the buzz around the watercooler after an episode of *Lost* or *Heroes*. Some of these buzzwords quickly pass, while others remain embedded in the language for years to come. Whether we're discussing the "truthiness" of the president's most recent press conference, chatting about the new "McDreamy" at the office, or merely exclaiming "D'oh!" after we've made a dumb mistake, there's no denying that TeleWords change the way we talk about entertainment—and about the wider world.

TOP 10 TELEWORDS OF 2007

This annual list captures the spirit of the times, for better or for worse. Themes, stars, and shows may change at an ever quickening pace, but this only reflects the world in which we live, more than we'd ever like to admit.

These TeleWords were nominated by GLM's language police, volunteer language observers scattered the world over. The words are then run through the Predictive Quantities Indicator (PQI), the proprietary algorithm that analyzes the global print and electronic media, the Internet, and blogosphere, and then ranks the words according to year by year change, acceleration, and directional momentum.

Here, then, are the top TeleWords of 2007:

SURGE (Iraq War): A military and political strategy, on the lips of every politician.

"THAT'S HOT!"® (Paris Hilton): Hilton owns the trademark to the phrase "That's hot," which was registered on February 13. What's next? Britney trademarking "public breakdown"?

"D'OH" (*The Simpsons*): As in "dough," as the Simpsons' leap to the silver screen grosses $485 million and counting.

BLACKOUT (*The Sopranos*): The series-ending episode redefined the word *cliffhanger* since there was no hanging about the cliff in any way, shape, or form, rather a sharp plunge into the abyss.

"YATTA!" (*Heroes*): Yatta! narrowly beats out "WTF is going to happen now?"

THE MCEMMYS (*Grey's Anatomy*): This show's cast and alumni (a.k.a. McDreamy, McSteamy, & Crew) always have a host of prime-time nominations.

"I LIKE TO HAVE THE ANSWERS BEFORE I ASK QUESTIONS." (*The Closer*): Kyra Sedgwick's trademark sassiness on display.

"No miniskirts after 35 . . ." (*What Not to Wear*): . . . nor white shoes after Labor Day. Stacy London and Clinton Kelly dissect fashion victims (and what led them to their present dire circumstance).

Scranton, or is it Wilkes-Barre? (*The Office*): The extended mockumentary is located in this gritty Northeast Pennsylvania city.

Oy vey! (*Criminal Minds*): Mandy Patinkin, as is his wont, deserts the set, yet again.

Bonus Words: *Peek, Copy, and Save* (*Are You Smarter Than a Fifth Grader?*): Solid advice for anyone, in most circumstances, especially after fifth grade.

THE TOP TELEWORDS OF THE RECENT PAST

Truthiness (*The Colbert Report*): Truth unencumbered by the facts.

Wikiality (*The Colbert Report*): Reality as determined by majority vote. First time ever with two words from the same show.

Katrina (the news): First TeleWord hit of the 2005–'06 season, unfortunately from a direct hit on New Orleans.

Katie (*CBS Evening News*): Katie Couric, whose move to nighttime news has everyone wondering about the state of her "gravitas."

Dr. McDreamy (*Grey's Anatomy*): Patrick Dempsey follows in a long line of television "dreamboat" physicians, dating back to Richard Chamberlain's Dr. Kildare from the *Dr. Kildare* show.

BUSH'S WAR (the news): Echoing the labels (e.g., Mr. Lincoln's war) bestowed upon wars waged by Presidents Lincoln, Wilson, Roosevelt, Truman, Johnson and Nixon in two centuries past.

MAN OF THE HOURS (*24*): Keifer Sutherland, from his real-time hit show.

OCD: Tony Sholub's OCD (obsessive-compulsive disorder) was a lesser-known disease going mainstream.

DYSFUNCTIONAL (*The Office*): The office as family. Dysfunctional family, that is.

FALLING STAR (*The View*): Rosie O'Donnell, in her recent battles with Donald Trump (and a host of others) on *The View* (produced by Barbara Walters).

REFUGEE (the news): From ongoing coverage of the devastation wrought by Hurricane Katrina. For millions, the word eventually took on a racial undertone and was subsequently replaced by *evacuee*, and others.

DESPERATION (*Desperate Housewives*, the news): *Desperate Housewives* began the television year in good fun but, as the year progressed, the world witnessed an ongoing war, a tsunami, the death of a beloved pope, and unprecedented destruction on the American Gulf Coast. Desperation, indeed.

CAMP CUPCAKE (the news): From the ongoing Martha Stewart follies, the minimum-security WV facility where Martha did her time. The campus was modeled after that of Bucknell University.

REALITY TV (*The Bachelor, Survivor, The Simple Life*, and the like): Real-world reality bested the manufactured kind by a long shot in recent television seasons.

CURMUDGEON (*House*): Acerbic, caustic, antisocial, and mean-spirited: these are the socially redeeming qualities of *House*'s brilliant physician.

"IT'S WHAT WE DO." (*Stargate SG-1*): In 2006 *Stargate SG-1* became the longest running sci-fi television series in the history of the medium. When asked what it's like to lead the SG-1 team to exotic worlds, Gen. Jack O'Neil always answers with this simple declaration.

BACKSTORY (*Lost*): This popular drama took the story-behind-the-story concept to the next level.

TSUNAMI (the news): Before a massive, earthquake-fueled wave took a quarter of a million South Asian lives, most of the viewing audience had only a vague acquaintance with the word.

MOBISODES: Not another season of the *Sopranos*, but one-minute TV episodes designed specifically for mobile media. Coming soon to a cell phone near you.

MORE TELEWORDS OF THE RECENT PAST

"YOU'RE FIRED!" (*The Apprentice*): Donald Trump's signature phrase.

MESS O' POTAMIA (*The Daily Show with Jon Stewart*): The Show's name for the ongoing military and political situation in the Middle East. Today, more eighteen-to forty-nine-year-olds get their news from *The Daily Show* than from mainstream news media.

GOD (*Joan of Arcadia* and *Angels in America*): The Supreme Being makes quite a comeback on the small screen.

WARDROBE MALFUNCTION: Originally from the Janet Jackson/Justin Timberlake incident at the Super Bowl when she (inadvertently?) bared her breast, reinforced by a plethora of ongoing incidents. Now used to describe any clothing mishap.

INFECTIOUS DISEASE (*CSI* franchise): Evidently nothing can contain the *CSI* franchise.

THE O.C.: From *The O.C.*, a show about living the upper middle class life in Southern California's Orange County. TV literally is a "geography of the mind."

EXTREME MAKEOVER: From the many and varied makeover shows (make over your life, your room, your husband, your kids, etc.) that have become a worldwide phenomenon. Both *extreme* and *makeover* made the list, in any combination.

GRIM REAPER: From the show *Dead Like Me*, about the goings-on of a crew of contemporary Grim Reapers. The G.R. hasn't made such an impact on popular culture since Ingmar Bergman's *Seventh Seal*.

WORDS THAT ARE NOTEWORTHY
BUT NO LONGER HIP

FAHGEDDABOUTIT! (*The Sopran*os): This expression came up in the everyday lives of the mob in North Jersey. Forget about Fahgeddaboutit!

VOTED OFF THE ISLAND: From the various incarnations of the long-running *Survivor* franchise. This phrase has been voted off the TeleWord List.

So (as an intensitve): From the long-running comedy *Friends*, about the dating (and mating) rituals of a group of friends in Manhattan. As in "That is *so* not fair." This adjective is *so* yesterday.

TOP TELEWORDS AND PHRASES OF YESTERYEAR

KEMOSABE: The Lone Ranger's partner, Tonto, called him Kemo Sabe, or "Faithful Friend."

THE MICKEY MOUSE CLUB: The famous Disney show that served as a springboard for generations of child actors into the limelight, and occasionally into stardom. Examples include Annette Funicello, Britney Spears, Christina Aguilera, and Justin Timberlake.

I LOVE LUCY: This show brilliantly brought screwball comedy to the small screen, as when Lucille Ball signs up as the Vita-meat-a-vegamin Girl and a legendary career is launched to new heights.

"GOOD NIGHT AND GOOD LUCK": The signature sign-off of Edward R. Murrow as he invented television news, just as "This . . . is London" was his signature sign-on from the rooftops of London during the Blitz. The phrase was brought back into the public eye after the success of George Clooney's film about the life of the famous newsman.

TUTTI-FRUITI ICE CREAM: America watched the Nelson family grow up on the small screen. You could always count on this staple of Ozzie and Harriet's diet to help straighten out life's problems.

"I AM PREPARED TO WAIT UNTIL HELL FREEZES OVER": Adlai Stevenson's words during the Nikita Khrushchev-Adlai Stevenson Debate at the United Nations in 1962, which epitomized the cold war antagonism. Also the origin of Khrushchev's "We will bury you" comment.

"GOOD NIGHT, MARY-ELLEN"—"GOOD NIGHT, JIM-BOB"—"GOOD NIGHT, ELIZABETH"—"GOOD NIGHT, BEN" . . . "GOOD NIGHT, JOHN-BOY": The ending of each episode of *The Waltons*, the show that perhaps optimized the term "family values."

GRASSHOPPER: From (*Kung Fu*): the name given by Master Po to the young Caine, inspired by the sounds of the grasshopper Master Po hears at Caine's feet.

"SOCK IT TO ME!" *Rowan and Martin's Laugh-In's* "Sock-it-to-me" Girl was replaced for a night by the future president of the United States, Richard M. Nixon.

"THE SIGNPOST UP AHEAD—YOUR NEXT STOP, THE TWILIGHT ZONE!" From the introduction to *The Twilight Zone*, Rod Serling's groundbreaking late 1950s series.

"FIRST STAR ON THE RIGHT AND STRAIGHT ON TILL TUESDAY": From Mary Martin's live performance as Peter Pan, which captivated a youthful '50s audience.

"PRESIDENT KENNEDY IS DEAD": The central television event of the last century; it took Walter Cronkite the better part of an hour to establish a phone line to Dallas.

"LADIES AND GENTLEMEN, THE BEATLES": Ed Sullivan. Few remember that the Lads from Liverpool burst upon the world's consciousness a mere ninety days after the Kennedy assassination.

TRICKY DICKIE: The world of politics has never been the same since Kennedy used the "coolness" of the medium to his great advantage—and Nixon's five o'clock shadow emphasized the "Tricky Dickie" sobriquet.

"AND THAT'S THE WAY IT IS": The signoff of Walter Cronkite, the dean of network news.

"AND LIVE FROM NEW YORK, IT'S SATURDAY NIGHT": *Saturday Night Live* has served as an incubator for future stardom: Chevy Chase, Gilda Radner, Billy Crystal, Jane Curtin, Mike Myers, Dennis Miller, Bill Murray, Chris Rock, John Belushi, and Adam Sandler, among many others.

"HERE'S JOHNNY!" Ed McMahon's introduction of the *Tonight Show*'s Johnny Carson over a two-decade reign. Appropriated by Jack Nicholson in the big-screen thriller *The Shining*.

"TO GO WHERE NO MAN HAS GONE BEFORE": The mission of Captain Kirk's Starship Enterprise on the

amazingly short-lived series *Star Trek*, which went on
to produce an astounding number of spin-offs.

CORONATION OF QUEEN ELIZABETH II: The English-
speaking world was enthralled by the spectacle, much
as it was four decades later by the marriage of her son,
Prince Charles, to a former Kindergarten teacher, Lady
Spenser (soon to be known as Princess Diana).

CelebWords

At a later point in his career, Einstein postulated what he termed
to be the Cosmological Constant, designated as the Greek letter
lambda (Λ). Though he ended up considering this to be one of the
great mistakes of his career, this turned out to be ever so important
to one of the greatest questions of twenty-first century cosmology
(the study of the Universe): Why do the galaxies, nebulae and stars
behave the way they do?

In the same way, I propose the existence of the Holly-
woodological Constant that—no matter what the crisis of the real
world (Tsunamis, war, starvation)—keeps the Hollywood stars at the
center of things.

Celebrity Children's Names

The children of the current crop of Hollywood stars will never
say their names are just names, not when these painstakingly con-
trived appendages have been bestowed upon them with much fan-
fare and media hype. This represents yet another Hollywood trend,
where the baby's name is seen as just another Hollywood adornment. Having children has become a fad, and like any fad emanat-
ing from Hollywood, self-augmentation, adornment, and going to
the extreme are blatantly apparent.

Suri

There are at least five meanings for "Suri," including the name of a Nubian tribe on the Sudanese-Ethiopian border. The tribe is known for the ceremonial clay plate inserted into the lower lip of Suri girls after their lower teeth have been extracted.

"Suri" also refers to the sun in Sanskrit, an ancient Indo-European language in which the word's meaning sometimes is translated as "lord" or "ruler."

Moreover, "Suri" is the name for the wool of the Andean Alpaca.

In Persian, it means "rose," though not necessarily a red rose, as Tom Cruise and Katie Holmes said through their spokesman when the birth was announced.

It is also a rare variation of the biblical name Sarah, which means "lady" or "princess."

Combined with the child's last name, which in English means to move or go along, especially in an unhurried or unconcerned fashion, Suri Cruise could translate to: "The ruling Nubian sun princess unhurriedly moving along wearing a rose-colored blanket."

Note: Things aren't so different in China where children during the late twentieth century were named with various words suggesting the beneficial leadership of Chairman Mao Zedong. Even now, there are instances where parents are attempting to use Internet words and symbols for names. In a recent case, a father was forbidden to name his son with the @ sign, since symbols are not allowed in Chinese names.

Suri, Shiloh Nouvel, and the rest of the Hollywood Babyland parade have opened an entire new world of possibilities to young parents, who are taking to the idea of bestowing (or inflicting?) outré names upon their children. On the other hand, though these names seem unusual now, two generations hence they just might be the Johns and Marys of their time.

Some of the oddest celebrity baby names follow.

RECENTLY NAMED CHILDREN
OF CELEBRITY PARENTS

Amber Rose Tamara, Saffron Sahara, and *Tallulah Pine:*
daughters of Simon LeBon and Yasmin Parvaneh

Apple and *Moses:* daughter and son of Gwyneth
Paltrow and Chris Martin

Audio Science: son of Shannyn Sossamon and Dallas
Clayton

Banjo Patrick: son of Rachel Griffiths and Andrew
Taylor

Bogart Che Peyote and *Rocco Kokopelli:* sons of David
"Puck" Rainey and Betty Rainey

BreAzia Ranee: daughter of Olympia Scott-Richardson
and Al Richardson

Brooklyn Joseph, Romeo James, and *Cruz David:* daughter and two sons of David and Victoria (Posh Spice)
Beckham

Denim Cole: son of Toni Braxton and Keri Lewis

Dusti Raine and *Keelee Breeze:* daughters of Robert Van
Winkle (Vanilla Ice) and Laura Giarritta

Dweezil, Ahmet Emuukha Rodan, Moon Unit, and *Diva
Muffin:* two sons and two daughters of Frank Zappa
and Gail Zappa

Elijah Blue: son of Cher and Greg Allman

Fifi Trixibelle, Peaches Honeyblossom, and *Little Pixie:*
daughters of Sir Bob Geldof and Paula Yates

Free: son of Barbara Hershey and David Carradine

Gaia Romilly: daughter of Emma Thompson and Greg Wise

George Jr., George II, George III, George IV, George V, George VI, Freeda George, and *Georgetta:* the six sons and two daughters of George Foreman

Heavenly Hiraani Tiger Lily: daughter of Michael Hutchence and Paula Yates

Hud and *Speck Wildhorse:* sons of John Cougar Mellencamp and Elaine Irwin

Isaiah Akin, Thyme, and *Imam:* sons and daughter of Isaiah Washington and Jenisa Marie Washington

Kal-El: son of Nicholas Cage and Alice Kim

Makena'lei Gordon: daughter of Helen Hunt and Matthew Carnahan

Moxie CrimeFighter: daughter of Penn Jillette and Emily Jillette

Phinnaeus and *Hazel:* son and daughter of Julia Roberts and Daniel Moder

Poppy Honey and *Daisy Boo:* daughters of Jamie and Juliette "Jools" Oliver

Puma: daughter of Erykah Badu and Tracy Curry

Reignbow and *Freedom:* daughter and son of Ving Rhames and Deborah Reed

"Rocket" Valentin, "Racer" Maximilliano, "Rebel" Antonio,

Rogue, and *Rhiannon:* four sons and one daughter of Robert Rodriguez and Elizabeth Avellan

Rufus Tiger, *Tiger Lily*, and *Lola Daisy:* son and two daughters of Roger Taylor and Deborah Leng

Rumer Glenn, *Scout Larue*, and *Tallulah Belle:* daughters of Bruce Willis and Demi Moore

Sage Moonblood and *Seargeoh:* daughter and son of Sylvester Stallone and Sasha Czack

Sailor Lee: daughter of Christie Brinkley and Peter Cook

Seven Sirius: son of Erykah Badu and André Benjamin.

Shiloh Nouvel, *Zahara Marley*, *Maddox Chivan Thornton*, and *Pax Thien:* daughter, son, daughter, and son of Brad Pitt and Angelina Jolie

Sophia Rose, *Sistine Rose*, and *Scarlet Rose:* daughters of Sylvester Stallone and Jennifer Flavin

Teddy Jo and *Justice:* daughters of John Cougar Mellencamp and Vicky Granucci

CHAPTER THREE

The Personal Is Political

How Politics and Current Events Shape Public Dialogue

Sometimes seemingly innocent words become politically "hot" through no fault of their own. Take, for example, a word that means "marsh" or a "quaking bog," the type that seems to tremble every time you take a step: *quagmire*. Since the Vietnam War, this word has been applied to any intractable situation, especially on the battlefield, such as the Iraq War. Critics of the conflict know that *quagmire* is a very powerful word, and that using it will engender powerful images of ongoing death and destruction. Supporters attempt to avoid use of the word, and try to replace it with words that suggest victory, nobility, patriotism, and the like. *Quagmire* was transformed from its original meaning to its current one carrying all the baggage of a hot political buzzword. How does this happen? Suffice to say, it takes a "perfect storm" of circumstances in the cultural milieu to transform "a lowland area, such as a marsh or swamp, that is saturated with moisture, especially when regarded as the natural habitat of wildlife" into a synonym for mayhem, death, and destruction from which it is impossible (or at least highly improbable) to extricate oneself.

Myth of the 24-Hour News Cycle

Although it is commonly assumed that the media is now on a 24-hour news cycle, the opposite appears to be true, according to our analysis at the Global Language Monitor. We've found that although day-to-day headlines are relatively transient, the ideas encapsulated in the political buzzwords that GLM tracks take several months to cycle through the electronic and print media, particularly when it comes to cyberspace and the blogosphere.

Once a politically sensitive buzzword is launched into today's media world, it persists for an indeterminate period, building a kind of media momentum and extending the news cycle. This persistence seems at odds with the general perception of the media being fixated on the 24-hour news cycle.

This chapter will show how hundreds of words and phrases have made this unlikely leap into the political vocabulary. It will also help you better understand what is happening the next time you see a word begin to appear in new and unusual contexts, as it is shaped into a new political buzzword.

Bushisms

When George W. Bush first stepped upon the world stage during the 2000 presidential primaries, it quickly became evident that the future president had an atypical relationship with the English language. Evidently, even the rigorous training one receives at Yale and Harvard did little to mollify the situation. (Who knows, it actually may have exacerbated it.) His conversation was sprinkled with words such as *resignate* and *misunderestimate*, and misuse of words like *Grecian*. Academia and the media howled.

Misunderestimated?

Attributed to President George W. Bush, *misunderestimated* was the Global Language Monitor Word of the Year for 2002. Used in place of the more straightforward *underestimated*, it can now be found with its many variations (for example, *misoverestimated*) hundreds of thousands of times on the Web.

This one looks like a keeper.

At GLM, we started tracking Bushisms from a different point of view: How do presidential "Bushisms" fare over time? Do they add to the language? Or are they just so much dust in the wind? Do they become mere ephemera, or worse: the subjects of late night humor, quickly to be forgotten?

So far it seems that some will stick, and some will be disregarded (probably for the best). Incidentally, *resignate* and *misunderestimate* were words that have been listed in unabridged dictionaries long before "W" mispronounced them.

TOP EARLY BUSHISMS (OR, CLASSIC BUSHISMS)

The following four words were selected in an online CNN poll embedded in an article about the Global Language Monitor's Selection Process. They are the perfect examples of classic Bushisms.

MISUNDERESTIMATE: To significantly underestimate.

EMBETTER: The opposite of embitter.

RESIGNATE: To resign oneself (actually dates from the seventeenth century).

FOREIGN-HANDED: To be adept at foreign policy.

A Warren G. Harding-ism *The word* hospital *has been in use since the days of the Roman Republic. However, its derivative,* hospitalization, *caused an uproar after President Warren G. Harding first used it in the early 1920s. You can now find it on the Internet over 10 million times.*

TOP 15 BUSHISMS, SECOND TERM

1. *"I'm the decider"*: "I'm the decider, and I decide what is best. And what's best is for Don Rumsfeld to remain as the secretary of defense." Some six months later, Rumsfeld was cited as one of the major reasons for the "thumpin'" (Bush's word) the Republicans received in the midterm elections. April 18, 2006. (Already, *Newsweek* has run an article about what type of "decider" the presidential candidates might be.)

2. *"I use the Google."* In reference to the popular search engine, October 24, 2006.

3. *"It was not always certain that the U.S. and America would have a close relationship."* June 29, 2006. At times, this seems frighteningly true.

4. *"I've got an ek-a-lec-tic reading list."* August 29, 2006.

5. *"The only way we can win is to leave before the job is done."* November 24, 2006.

6. *"Stay the course."* On a multitude of occasions.

7. *"When the final history is written on Iraq, it will look just like a comma."* September 24, 2006.

8. *"The Congress was right to renew the Terrorist Act."* In reference to the Patriot Act, September 7, 2006.

9. *"I want to be a war president; no president wants to be a war president."* October 26, 2006.

10. *"The fiscal year that ended on February the 30th."* The government fiscal year ends on September 30, and there is no February 30. (There actually was a February 30, and a February 29, on the calendar, until the emperors Julius Caesar and Augustus Caesar took them and added days to their namesake months, July and August.) October 1, 2006.

11. *"Brownie, you're doing a heck of a job."* To FEMA director Michael Brown, who resigned ten days later amid criticism over his handling of the Katrina recovery efforts, September 2, 2005.

12. *"See, in my line of work you got to keep repeating things over and over and over again for the truth to sink in, to kind of catapult the propaganda."* Explaining his communications strategy, May 24, 2005.

13. *"I think I may need a bathroom break. Is this possible?"* A note to Secretary of State Condoleezza Rice during a UN Security Council meeting, September 14, 2005.

14. *"This notion that the United States is getting ready to at-*

tack Iran is simply ridiculous. And having said that, all options are on the table." February 22, 2005.

15. *"In terms of timetables, as quickly as possible—whatever that means."* On his time frame for Social Security legislation, March 16, 2005.

Bonus: *"Those who enter the country illegally violate the law":* On illegal immigrants or undocumented workers, November, 28, 2005.

OTHER PRESIDENTS' BUSHISMS

Both the press and the public have given George W. Bush a hard time about his inventiveness with the English language. But once we started looking, we were surprised by how many common words used today (hospitalization, muckraker, administration, OK) were actually coined by former presidents' verbal gaffes. And the third U.S. president, Thomas Jefferson, was said to have coined some one hundred new words—intentionally. Here are some other presidential neologisms, either coined or made popular by past commanders in chief.

Administration (George Washington)

Belittle (Thomas Jefferson)

Breadstuff (Thomas Jefferson)

Bully pulpit (Theodore Roosevelt)

Caucus (John Adams)

Countervailing (Thomas Jefferson)

Muckraker (Theodore Roosevelt)

Normalcy (Woodrow Wilson)

O.K. (Martin Van Buren)

Sanction (Thomas Jefferson)

"Swift Boats" and "Moral Values": The Impact of the Election Season on Our Vocabulary

The lead-up to a presidential election always highlights an eclectic group of words and phrases. Some originate with the candidates themselves, while others are emphasized by talking heads and reporters. In the future I have no doubt that new words and phrases will be brought to the forefront since American presidential campaigns are, perhaps, the quintessential examples of the free-market economy, with all the unabashed boosterism, hucksterism, and mudslinging that this implies.

I'm OK, You're OK: The most understood word on the planet

Have you ever wondered why *OK* consists of two capital letters? President Martin Van Buren (AD 1837–1841) was born in Old Kinderhook, New York. His nickname, Old Kinderhook, was incorporated into his campaign slogan ("Old Kinderhook is O.K."), and O.K. Democratic Clubs sprung up around the young nation.

Alternative derivations, since disproved, suggested that *OK* was from the Greek phrase *ola kala* ("all well"), used in the shipping industry. Another, favored by President Woodrow Wilson, was that *OK* was derived from the Choctaw *okeh* (also meaning "all well"). The fact that *OK* is sometimes written as *O.K.* seems to tilt the argument in Old Kinderhook's favor, since when we write initials for any person, we usually write them in capital letters separated by periods. What is certain is that the U.S. presidential election of 1840—in which Van Buren was overwhelmingly defeated—secured *OK*'s growing usage and subsequent global expansion during the twentieth century.

OK?

Political Buzzwords of the 2008 Presidential Campaign

This disparate collection of buzzwords speaks volumes about today's electorate. We have an Iraq War strategy, a name, a corporate entity, and a commentary on a female candidate's neckline at the top of the list . . . and then it really gets interesting. Political buzzwords are terms or phrases that become loaded with emotional freight beyond the normal meaning of the word. For example, the word *surge* has been in the English-language vocabulary since time immemorial. However, in its new context as an Iraq War strategy, it inspires a set of emotions in many people far beyond the norm. Using its PQI Index, GLM was the only media analytics organization that foresaw the '04 electorate voting with their moral compasses rather than their pocketbooks.

Not a Shred of Truth *Actually, it's not a shard of truth. Truth, by its very nature, does not shred. In ancient Athens, broken pottery was evidently everywhere in the streets, pieces of which were called shards. Citizens would use the shards as notepaper. They would also use them to vote, by marking shards. Over time, people forgot exactly what a shard was, so shred seemed the more likely word.*

THE TOP 10 POLITICAL BUZZWORDS OF THE 2008 PRESIDENTIAL CAMPAIGN

1. *Surge:* The "Surge" surges to the number one political buzzword; recently co-opted as "surge of hope."

2. *Obama:* His name now qualifies as a buzzword. This is quite unusual, though the name Hillary comes close.

3. *YouTube:* Changing the nature of American campaigning?

4. *Cleavage:* Despite critics' contentions, Hillary was found to be a woman after all.

5. *Pardon:* The furor over Scooter Libby's presidential pardon riled the news media.

6. *Live Earth:* Rock the Earth lived up to its billing in "buzz."

7. *Subpoena:* Congressional subpoenas abound as predicted if a Democratically controlled Congress were elected.

8. *Congress:* Congress is now polling lower numbers than the president. Congress as a dirty word; yet another 'c' word?

9. *All-time low:* A constant description of the president's ever falling poll numbers.

10. *"I don't recall"*: Former U.S. attorney general Alberto Gonzales used this phrase three score and thrice in but one day of testimony before Congress.

The Top Political Buzzwords for 2006 included throes, quagmire, credibility, global warming, *and* insurgency.

PQI RANKING OF POLITICAL BUZZWORDS ON NOVEMBER 6, 2006

Using the Predictive Quantities Indicator, we deconstructed the mind-set of the electorate immediately before the midterm elections. Candidates for the 2008 general election would be wise to consider this unlikely combination of concerns.

1. Ethanol
2. Global warming
3. Al Qaeda
4. Bird flu
5. Iran nuclear weapon
6. Impeach Bush
7. Conservative politics
8. Kerry "stuck in Iraq"
9. Increased tax revenue
10. Mark Foley scandal
11. Saddam Hussein execution
12. Raise taxes
13. Illegal immigration
14. Progressive politics
15. Climate change disaster
16. Liberal politics
17. Religious right

18. Cut taxes

19. Rumsfeld resign

20. Culture of corruption

21. Osama bin Laden

22. Domestic spying

23. Republican majority

24. Quagmire Iraq War

25. Extreme right political

26. Hillary Clinton credibility

27. Bush lame duck

28. Filibuster Senate

29. Iraq War insurgency

30. New Orleans recovery

31. Religious left

32. China world stage

33. Losing war Iraq

34. War for oil

35. George Bush credibility

36. Nuclear option Senate

37. Out of the political mainstream

38. Supreme Court nomination

39. Democratic majority

40. FEMA New Orleans

41. Nuclear weapon North Korea

42. NSA eavesdrop

43. Likeability Bush

44. Winning war in Iraq

45. Gasoline crisis

If the bulk of this list remains in the news, both Democrats and Republicans should focus on these issues. Perhaps a green party strong on national security would better represent the mood reflected in the current PQI than the currently available political options?

The Ship of State Flounders *Actually, ships do not flounder, that is, flop around like a fish. Rather, they run aground, or* founder, *on a sand bar.* Founder *is actually from the Latin* fundere, *meaning "to pour" (as in concrete) or "to set a foundation" (as in a building).* Flounder *is now more frequently used in this context than is the more proper* founder.

TOP POLITICAL BUZZWORDS OF THE 2004 PRESIDENTIAL CAMPAIGN

COLOSSAL ERROR: Kerry's judgment of Bush's Iraq policy.

FLIP-FLOP/FLOPPING: Formerly used only when referring to gymnastic routines, pancakes, or dolphin acts (Flipper), this label—denoting a sudden reversal of position—quickly became a mainstream political term.

GIRLIE MEN: California Governor Arnold Schwarzenegger's (a.k.a. "the Governator") characterization of political opponents, a phrase originally used to mock him on *Saturday Night Live*. In this case, a TeleWord became a political buzzword.

GLOBAL TEST: Kerry's description of the requirements he'd insist upon meeting before committing the United States to preemptive military strikes.

INCURIOSITY: Applied to the president (Incurious George) at the outset of the presidential campaign.

LIBERAL: Originally a positive political term referring to an ideology of individual rights, it is now looked upon as a pejorative. For future reference, please use *progressive*, which has come to mean the same thing without the negative connotations.

MARY CHENEY: For better or worse, Vice President Cheney's daughter became a household name in the six weeks leading up to the election.

MEDIA BIAS: The claim, made by Democrats and Republicans alike, that the media was partisan in its coverage of the election. The term came on strong in the wake of Dan Rather's *60 Minutes* imbroglio.

MISLEADER: As in "misleader in chief." Moveon.org was the originator of this epithet for the sitting president.

MORAL VALUES: Found in more than four-thousand media stories at the time of the election; its meaning is open to interpretation.

QUAGMIRE: A fading, Vietnam-era term rescued from obscurity. Originally "quaking" or "shaky" ground or mire, it was used to describe the situation in Iraq.

RED STATES/BLUE STATES: Before November 2, 2004, a relatively unknown shorthand used by political pundits. Now common parlance to describe Republican-leaning states vs. Democrat-leaning states.

RUSH TO WAR: A pejorative used by administration opponents to describe the run-up to the Iraq war. There was a period when the phrase was used in many articles in the same newspaper or television broadcast on a daily basis.

SWIFT BOATS: Also known as Patrol Craft Fast (PCF), these shallow-water boats used during the Vietnam War may well have torpedoed Kerry's presidential aspirations.

TWO AMERICAS: John Edwards's frequent evocation of an America divided between rich and poor, jobless and the employed, liberals (er, progressives) and conservatives.

The World of PC Words

In 2006, the Political Correctness movement continued to gain momentum, inserting itself into ordinary English-language conversations across the country. But in addition to adding new, politically correct words to the language, the movement has also drawn our attention to the politically *incorrect* ones. Which, much of the time, are a lot more interesting to study.

THE TOP 10 POLITICALLY INCORRECT WORDS OF RECENT YEARS

1. *Macaca*: The use of an offensive slang term for Indians of the Subcontinent in the West Indies might have changed the political balance of the U.S. Senate, since George Allen's (R-VA) utterance surely impacted his election bid.

2. *Global warming denier:* There is now a proposal that global warming deniers be treated the same as holocaust deniers: professional ostracism, belittlement, ridicule, and even jail.

Terrorist or Bomber?

The BBC's use of the terms *misguided criminals* and *bombers* when referring to the perpetrators of the London Tube bombings stirred an international debate on politically correct language. (The BBC actually challenged GLM in a published article, disputing GLM's claim of the BBC's published policy of shying away from the word terrorist. GLM responded by providing a link to the BBC's policy.) The words replaced the term *terrorist*, which according to the BBC can "carry emotional or value judgments."

But according to the Global Language Monitor's PQ Index, the term *terrorist* appears 700 percent more frequently on the Web than does *bomber* when linked to terror-related activities such as suicide bombings and the like. When tracking global news articles only, the word *bomber* can be found in about 40 percent of the articles, though usually in combination with *terrorist* or *terrorist*-related words. The phrase *misguided criminals* is found only about five thousand times on the entire web.

3. *Herstory: Herstory* again attempts to take the male element out of *his*tory. Although there are nearly 900,000 Google citations for *herstory*, they are all based on a mistaken assumption. When Herodotus wrote the first history, the word meant simply an "inquiry."

4. *Flip chart:* The term *flip* can be offensive to Filipinos, who consider it an ethnic insult. California has issued sensitivity guidelines to avoiding using the term *flip chart* for easel pads or writing blocks.

5. *1a and 1b:* The headmistress of a grade school in Midlothian (Scotland) had to split a grade into two equal classes. Though the split was purely alphabetical, parents objected because those with children in "1b" feared they may be perceived as academically inferior to those in "1a."

6. *Black coffee:* Staff at a coffee shop in Glasgow refused to serve a customer who had ordered a "black coffee," believing it to be "racist." He wasn't served until he changed his order to "coffee without milk."

7. *Oriental: Asian*, please. Though this is generally a purely American phenomenon. In Europe, Asians prefer the term *Oriental*, which literally means "those from the East."

8. *Menaissance:* The rise of a "manliness" culture or male renaissance. Replaces *metrosexual*, which evidently appealed to women but not to men.

9. *Momtini:* A Michigan mom invented the term *momtini*—a cocktail consumed by a mother—as an act of rebellion against "parental correctness." This has raised the hackles of child protection and anti-alcohol groups.

PC Culture Running Globally Amok: Australia Bans the Word *Mate*!?

In 2005, the Department of Parliamentary Services in Canberra issued a general warning to its security staff, banning the use of the word *mate* in any dealings they might have with members of the Parliament or the public. Almost immediately, Australian prime minister John Howard called the ban "absurd," while the opposition labeled it "un-Australian." The ban has since been rescinded.

In direct response, the Global Language Monitor polled its readers (and inquired of its language police) for further suggestions of slang words and informal language that should be banned in Australia, to serve the public interest. To make the list, words had to be innocuous in themselves but, in the context of political correctness, potentially offensive to some segment of the populace.

10. *"Our Mother and Father who are in Heaven"*: From a new, "inclusive" Bible translation (*The Bible in a More Just Language*) that replaced what it believed to be "divisive" teachings of Christianity. The word *art*, I guess, was pulling people apart.

Bonus: *Political Correctness: Equality Essentials*, a training manual book used for staff training courses at Kirklees Council in West Yorkshire, suggests that the term *political correctness* is now politically incorrect.

A LIST OF FUTHER AUSTRALIAN SLANG TERMS AND COLLOQUIALISMS FIT TO BE AVOIDED, SHUNNED, OR OTHERWISE BANNED

BARBECUE: The shortened form, *barbie*, can be an invidious reference to the Barbie doll, and hence sexist.

ABSO-BLOODY-LUTELY: Though the term *bloody* can signify an intensive, this use can also heighten insensitivity to the plight of farm animals.

DOWN UNDER: *Down Under* signifies the existence of an Up Over, which obviously is in the superior position of Upness. Might make some residents feel inferior.

G'DAY: Some etymologists believe that *good* can be ultimately traced to an earlier word for *God*. Hence, *G'day*—a shortened form of "Good Day"—can represent a conspiracy to insinuate the theistic worldview into everyday life.

MATE: Originally used by classmates at male boarding schools. Obviously sexist, also elitist.

NAPPY: "Diaper." Might offend narcoleptics.

NAUGHT: The number zero. If this caught on, the English-speaking world might adopt a potentially offensive name for the first decade of the twenty-first century: the Naughties.

NO WORRIES: This is offensive to those with OCD, and to others who are plagued by constant self-doubt and apprehension.

Plonk: Inexpensive wine (in the United State it's called Ripple). *Plonk* is perhaps a contraction of *vin blanc*; this might offend Francophones.

Ta: "Thank you." In the spirit of international harmony, the French *s'il vous plait* is preferred.

Vegemite: Clearly a plot to foist the utopian ideal of a meatless sandwich upon a defenseless world.

Zed: The letter *z*. Not exactly slang, but a candidate for banishment nonetheless on general principles.

POLITICALLY CORRECT WORDS AND PHRASES

As we bend over backward to avoid offending our fellow men (and womyn!), some surprising phrases have crept into the language. The coded way we occasionally speak about war, gender, and politics shows either an increased sensitivity toward other people, or an increased fear of being branded tactless. For better or worse, these politically correct words and phrases look like they're here to stay.

Misguided criminals: The BBC's "neutral" term to describe those who carried out the bombings in the London Tube. The professed intent of these *misguided criminals* was to kill, without warning, as many innocents as possible—which is the common definition of *terrorist*.

Intrinsic aptitude (or lack thereof): Used by Lawrence Summers, the former president of Harvard University, to explain why women might be underrepresented in engineering and science.

THOUGHT SHOWER OR WORD SHOWER: A substitute for *brainstorm*, used to avoid offending those with brain disorders such as epilepsy.

OUT OF THE MAINSTREAM: Used to describe the ideology of one's political opponents. But consider this: At one time, slavery was in the mainstream, having your blood sucked out by leeches was in the mainstream, and thinking the sun orbited the earth was in the mainstream.

DEFERRED SUCCESS: A euphemism for *failure*. The Professional Association of Teachers in the United Kingdom considered a proposal to replace any notion of failure with *deferred success*, to bolster students' self-esteem.

WOMYN: Used in place of *woman* to distance the word from *man*. In fact, *man* is gender neutral in both the original Indo-European sense and in contemporary usage, such as *mankind* and *humankind*.

CE: There is a growing movement to replace AD (*anno Domini*, Latin for "Year of our Lord"), used in the West since the fifth century, with the ostensibly more neutral CE (Common Era).

DEVICE/CAPTURED DEVICE: Formerly known as *master/slave*, this computer networking protocol describes a device or process that has captured and involuntarily controls one or more other devices or processes.

NON-SAME-SEX MARRIAGE: The preferred term for gay *marriage* in Democratic presidential primaries. A quirky example of a "retronym."

AD 2008 or 2008 CE?

A small but vocal element is voicing opposition to the traditional Western practice of measuring events as occurring before or after the birth of Jesus, or BC and AD.

GLM's survey has found that in the worldwide electronic and print media the current convention of AD and BC is nearly fifty times as prevalent as that of CE and BCE. Nevertheless, the fact that the newer designations are now found at all indicates significant inroads where until recently none existed.

The CE and BCE conventions were introduced about a century ago in the Jewish and scientific communities, but now have been adopted increasingly by those who want to obscure the Judeo-Christian roots of Western civilization. The issue has become particularly polarizing on college campuses, at school textbook publishers, and in the various religious communities.

As with most language-based PC issues, the battle is intense, but no authority or group can mandate linguistic change. And the fact is that both CE and AD acknowledge the centrality of Jesus to the Western calendar, since both AD and CE refer to the birth of Jesus as the central time marker for the West.

WAITRON: A waiter or waitress. *Waitress* was considered sexist.

RED SOX LOVER: A Yankee hater, during the ALCS playoffs.

HIGHER POWER: God.

PROGRESSIVE: The new word for *liberal*, with fewer of the now-standard derogatory undertones.

INCURIOUS: A kinder word than some of the more impolite invectives for President Bush (such as *idiot* or *moron*).

INSURGENTS: A.k.a. *terrorists*, in Iraq.

BARISTA: Another term for *waitron*, popular in the coffee shop environment.

FIRST-YEAR STUDENT: A gender-neutral version of *Freshman*, though *Frosh* is still acceptable.

The Apocalypse Is Here: How Hurricane Katrina Influenced the English Language

The enormous impact of Hurricane Katrina on the United States' political and social landscape is undeniable, and sobering. The tragedy also had a huge effect on the PQI. The word "Katrina"

Mother Love Mistaken for Mother Subjugation, in an Effort to Be PC

A director of engineering for a Fortune 100 company in Chicago told of a new Human Resources executive being taken on a tour of the server room. The executive asked why all the machines bore names of women. The director explained that the machines were all named after the engineers'—who were both male and female—mothers. A few days later, a memo was circulated forbidding the practice. The HR executive felt that it was insulting to women to be associated with the word *server*. She obviously missed the point, that the server room was the exact opposite of what she supposed. In fact, the server room was the control center of a mighty global network.

has broken the all-time PQ Index record for citations (previously held by *pope* after the death of Pope John Paul II), and it has remained on the list of top political buzzwords ever since.

As coverage of the Hurricane Katrina disaster in the American Gulf States unfolded, GLM found that the worldwide media was awash in apocalyptic-type terminology. The ominous references included: disaster, biblical, global warming, Hiroshima, nuclear bomb, catastrophe, holocaust, apocalypse, and end-of-the-world.

These alarmist references appeared across the entire spectrum of the media, from the most reputable newspapers to the blogosphere to everywhere in between. The world appeared stunned that the only remaining superpower had been humbled, on its own soil, by the forces of nature. The global media was mesmerized by the event itself, as well as by the inability of the authorities to keep their own people fed, sheltered, evacuated, and alive, and their language reflected their moods.

According to GLM's analysis, here are the most frequently used terms associated with Hurricane Katrina in the global media:

DISASTER: The most common, and perhaps neutral, description. Literally "against the stars," in Latin.

Refugee vs. Evacuee

GLM's analysis found that the term *refugees*—usually associated with displaced persons in such places as the Sudan and Afghanistan—appeared five times more frequently in the global media than did the more neutral *evacuees*. This was cited as racially motivated by some of the black leadership. Accordingly, most of the major media outlets in the United States eliminated the usage of the word *refugees*, with a few exceptions (most notably, the *New York Times*).

"Disaster bares divisions of race and class across the Gulf states." (*Toronto Globe and Mail*)

BIBLICAL: Used as an adjective. Referring to the scenes of death, destruction, and mayhem chronicled in the Bible. "[A] town of 6,800 where corpses lie amid a scene of Biblical devastation." (*The Times*, London)

GLOBAL WARMING: The idea that the hand of man was directly responsible for the catastrophe, as opposed to the more neutral perpetrator, climate change. "German environmental minister Jürgen Trittin remains stolid in his assertion that Hurricane Katrina is linked to global warming and America's refusal to reduce emissions." (*Der Spiegel*)

HIROSHIMA/NUCLEAR DESTRUCTION: Fresh in the mind of the media, following the sixtieth anniversary of the Hiroshima and Nagasaki bombings. "Struggling with what he calls Hurricane Katrina's nuclear destruction, Mississippi Governor Haley Barbour shows the emotional strain of leading a state through a disaster of biblical proportions." (Associated Press)

CATASTROPHE: Sudden and often disastrous overturning, ruin, or undoing of a system. "In the Face of Catastrophe, Sites Offer Helping Hands." (*Washington Post*)

HOLOCAUST: Because of historical association, the word is seldom used to refer to death brought about by natural causes. "December's Asian catastrophe should have elevated 'tsunami' practically to the level of 'holocaust' in the world vocabulary, implying a loss of life beyond compare, and as callous as this might make us seem, Katrina was many things, but 'our tsunami' she wasn't." (*Henderson Dispatch* [NC])

APOCALYPSE: Referring to prophetic visions of the imminent destruction of the world, as found in the Book of Revelations. " 'Call it apocalyptic. Whatever you want to call it, take your pick. There were bodies floating past my front door,' said Robert Lewis, who was rescued as floodwaters invaded his home." (Reuters)

END OF THE WORLD: End-time scenarios that presage the Apocalypse. "This is like time has stopped. It's like the end of the world." (*Columbus Dispatch*)

Then there were those in the media calling Katrina a direct intervention of the hand of an angry or vengeful God, though one not necessarily aligned with America's enemies. In *Al-Siyassa* (Kuwait), Muhammad Yousef al-Mlaifi, director of the Kuwaiti Ministry of Endowment's research center, said "The terrorist Katrina is one of the soldiers of Allah, but not an adherent of al Qaeda."

KATRINA BUZZWORDS EXPLAINER

Whether God was involved or not, Katrina was a terrible tragedy that affected countless people. As a service to the public and the global media, the Global Language Monitor compiled the Katrina Buzzwords Explainer to help everyone understand the many local peoples, landmarks, traditions, and customs of the Hurricane-devastated area.

ACADIANS: French-speaking people who were expelled from Nova Scotia exactly 250 years ago and settled in the bayou. Subject of the epic poem *Evangeline*, by Henry Wadsworth Longfellow. See *Cajun*.

ARMY CORPS OF ENGINEERS: The USACE is responsible for investigating, developing, and maintaining the nation's water and related environmental resources.

ASTRODOME: The first enclosed stadium in the United States, in Houston; refugees from the Superdome in New Orleans were transported 350 miles to the Astrodome.

BAYOU: The area of swamp and marshlands surrounding New Orleans; home of Cajun culture.

BIG EASY: The nickname for the city of New Orleans, from the laid-back lifestyle one once found there. Other nicknames include, Crescent City, Fat City and N'Awlins.

BREACH: Sudden overpowering of a levee or a floodwall, allowing water to seep or rush in.

CAJUN: A corruption of the word "Acadian", literally a Louisianan who descends from French-speaking Acadians.

CATEGORY: The intensity of a hurricane, determined using various measurements such as the velocity of sustained wind. Categories range from 1 (weakest) to 5 (strongest). Katrina peaked at Category 4 and hit New Orleans as a Category 3 storm.

CLIMATE CHANGE: The warming of the Earth's atmosphere due to natural cycles (politically sensitive; believed to be primarily outside the control of man). See *Global warming*.

CREOLE: Derives from the Latin *creare*, meaning "to create." By the nineteenth century, black, white, and mixed-ancestry Louisianans used the term to distinguish themselves from foreign-born and Anglo-American settlers.

CYCLONE: A developing tropical storm, rotating counterclockwise in the Northern Hemisphere or clockwise in the Southern Hemisphere. Often confused with a tornado.

EYE: The center of the hurricane, where the skies are clear and the wind is nearly calm.

FEMA: Federal Emergency Management Agency, a branch of the U.S. Homeland Security Department. FEMA coordinates the U.S. federal government's response to national disasters.

FLOATING CASINOS: Casinos located along the now devastated Mississippi coast. They had brought an annual average revenue of $2.7 billion a year to the state.

FLOOD CONTROL: The building of levees, pumping stations, sea walls, etc., to keep a city safe from flooding. In this case, a false hope for a city sitting several meters below sea level (and sinking still).

FLOOD STAGE: The point at which a rising river or tide becomes a flood.

FLOOD WALL: Narrow steel-and-concrete barrier erected to keep the Mississippi River out of New Orleans.

FRENCH QUARTER: The original living area of the city, now known for jazz, Cajun cuisine, and Carnival. Located at the highest point of the city.

GLOBAL WARMING: The warming of Earth's atmosphere, caused primarily by human use of fossil fuels (politically sensitive; believed to be primarily in the control of man). See *Climate change*.

HURRICANE: A tropical cyclone with a sustained surface wind of 74 mph (118 kmh) or more. A hurricane is called a "typhoon" in the Pacific Ocean.

HURRICANE NAMES: Hurricanes have been named since 1953. Currently, the World Meteorological Organization maintains the alphabetically sorted list of alternating men's and women's names. The list was exclusively female until 1979. Names are recycled every six years. Influential hurricanes have their names retired.

HURRICANE SCALE: See *Category*.

HURRICANE SEASON: The hurricane season in the Atlantic runs from June 1 to November 30; in the Eastern Pacific, the season begins on May 15 and ends on November 30.

ISOBAR: Isobars around a cyclone are lines on a map that signify the same barometric pressure.

KATRINA: The eleventh tropical storm of the 2005 Atlantic hurricane season. Name since retired.

KNOT: Wind speed equal to 1.15 miles per hour (mph) or 1.9 kilometers per hour (km/hr).

LAKE PONTCHARTRAIN—Actually, an arm of the sea that borders on New Orleans. Lake Pontchartrain is half the size of the state of Rhode Island.

LEVEE: Colossal earthen barriers erected to keep water out of the city. Once breached, levees hinder relief efforts by holding the water inside the city. New Orleans has 350 miles of hurricane levees; they were supposedly built to withstand a fast moving Category 3 storm.

NATIONAL GUARD: Military units organized at the state level to protect the citizens of an individual state.

NORLINS: Local pronunciation of "New Orleans."

PUBLIC HEALTH EMERGENCY: Cholera and typhoid—caused by contaminated water—were among the health concerns after Katrina.

PUMPING STATIONS: Massive, old, and inefficient pump houses that would supposedly keep any seepage out of New Orleans.

RECOVERY: To recover the dead after search-and-rescue operations are complete.

RELIEF AND RESPONSE EFFORT: To provide food, medical supplies, and shelter to evacuees of a disaster.

SAFFIR-SIMPSON SCALE: Used to give an estimate of potential damage and flooding along the coast. Wind speed is the determining factor in the scale. See *Category*.

SANDBAG: In this case, three thousand– to twenty thousand–pound burlap-type containers, dropped from Chinook helicopters to plug breaches in a levee.

SEARCH AND RESCUE: The people sent to search for survivors.

STORM SURGE: Sudden rising of the sea over its usual level, preceding the arrival of a hurricane. The thirty-foot surge on the Mississippi coastline before Katrina was the highest ever recorded in North America.

SUPERDOME: Home to the New Orleans Saints football team, the Sugar Bowl, and numerous Super Bowls, this sports venue became the nearly unbearable way station for many of the city's stranded.

TROPICAL DEPRESSION: An area of intense thunderstorms that becomes organized into a cyclone. Maximum sustained winds reach 34 knots (39 mph). There is at least one "closed" isobar, with a decrease in barometric pressure in the center of the storm. A level of intensity below a tropical storm.

TROPICAL STORM: A storm that begins to look like a hurricane, with sustained wind speeds up to 64 knots (73 mph).

VERTICAL EVAC: Vertical evacuation, taking refuge in the top floors of a highrise building. In this case, vertical evacuation often proved fatal.

With a few notable exceptions, every era (and every nation) seems to think that its era is unique in history, and that how things are ordered now is how things always were (and always will be). This is especially true in the West, where two-thousand years ago Rome was called "the Eternal City," the Romans having conveniently forgotten that a few hundred years before the reign of the Caesars, Roma was a quaint village on the banks of the river Tiberus.

And so it is with the intermixing of politics and language. Politicians' and the media's rather primitive attempts to shape the language in the name of politics cease to be outrageous, obscene, and incorrect, and the words and phrases they've created conveniently transform themselves into a part of Global English. And then we forget that they ever meant anything different.

CHAPTER FOUR

Study Abroad

How Foreign Languages and Worldwide English Speakers Are Transforming the English Language

As English becomes an ever more global language, it is becoming increasingly common for local derivations, offshoots and neologisms to congeal into a sort of local English-language stew. Linguists call this admixture a "patois," not a dialect, but certainly a distinct subsegment of the language. Rather new to this scene is the emergence of what I call the "lishes." A score or more of these lishes are springing up around the planet and are one of the many sources contributing to the growth of Global English. Some of the more prominent lishes are Chinglish (Chinese-English), Hinglish (Hindi-English), and Spanglish (Spanish-English) among many others.

Chinese + English = Chinglish

With some 250 million Chinese people either currently learning to speak English or already fluent, there will soon be more English speakers in China than in the entire British Commonwealth. And because such an immense number of Chinese are studying and speaking the language, the impact (and imprint) upon English cannot be denied. Many of the new English words registered on the Global Language Monitor's databases every year are influenced by the Chinese, and that number is bound to keep growing

Since each Chinese ideogram can have many meanings and interpretations, translating Chinese ideas into English is, indeed, extremely difficult. Because of this, Chinese-English hybrid words are often viewed with amusement by the rest of the English-speaking world. Nevertheless, this abundance of new words and phrases, unlikely as it may seem, is one of the prime drivers of the globalization of the English language. And as Global English evolves through the twenty-first century, Chinglish will, undoubtedly, continue to have a sizable impact.

Of course, a language can best be viewed as a living entity, which grows just like any other living thing and is shaped by the environment in which it lives. With the continuing emergence of China on the world stage, perhaps best exemplified by the Beijing Olympics, the Chinese state is now attempting to stamp out some of the more egregious examples of Chinglish. There have even been recent reports of university students systematically combing through major cities, neighborhood by neighborhood, visiting merchants, shops and restaurants looking for the offending Chinglish phrases and suggesting alternatives. But if the past is any example, they will have a most difficult time succeeding.

I've listed some of the more egregious Chinglish phrases below.

THE TOP 5 CHINGLISH WORDS AND PHRASES

1. *No noising:* "Quiet please!" Very logical, don't you think?

2. *Airline pulp:* Airline food. Their term, in this case, might be more appropriate than ours.

3. *Jumping umbrella:* Hang-glider. But a jumping umbrella sounds more interesting!

4. *Question authority:* Information booth. Not Chairman Mao's preferred translation.

5. *Burnt meat biscuit:* Bread dipped in a savory meat sauce. Not something you eat when visiting Scottish friends in the Australian Outback.

Bonus: GLM's all-time favorite, from previous surveys, is *The slippery are very crafty:* Slippery when wet! This one transcends the original intent.

THE TOP CHINGLISH WORDS AND PHRASES OF THE RECENT PAST (OR, CHINGLISH CLASSICS)

DEFORMEDMAN: "A public toilet for the disabled." Certainly politically incorrect by Western standards.

DON'T SHOW YOUR ENGLISH! "Stop showing off!" Speaking proper English is now a competitive sport.

INTERWANG: "Internet." From *wang*, meaning "fishing net" or "emperor."

ENGINEROOM: "Important person." In the *interwang* world, the high priests are those who emerge from the holy of holies: the engineer's room.

GREENFUD: "Organic food." Not to be confused with *green cheese*, the putative composition of the moon.

HAND LADDER: "Escalator." Derived from the need to hold your child's hand while ascending or descending.

SLIPPERCRAFTY: "Treacherously icy road." Both crafty and slippery in the highly negative sense.

DRINKTEA: "I'm taking a break; the store will reopen shortly." Origin self-explanatory.

WELCOMEAGAIN: "Thank you." Similar to the Hawaiian *aloha* but more specific: "We look forward to welcoming you again into our store."

Long Time No See *The oft-used expression "long time no see" is a word-for-word Chinese to English translation, first noted in the western United States in the mid 1800s.*

China Confronts Its Future

China has recently acknowledged the winds of change as the Ministry of Education (MOE) admitted some 171 neologisms into the Chinese language. Words were considered only after they passed the scrutiny of a dozen scholars associated with the Chinese Academy of Social Sciences (CASS) Institute of Linguistics. The academy had assembled a database of nearly one billion words gathered from the print and electronic media and then analyzed the new words that appeared most frequently. The official who is responsible for standardizing contemporary Chinese told the Beijing media that the "new coinages reflect rapid cultural and social changes in recent years as well as thriving new concepts in our daily lives." Therefore, not all terms were admitted, no matter how frequently they were found. These include *cool*, *zip it*, 3Q (for "thank you"), and *kick your ass*. For these terms, Chinese citizens will have to resort to the original English.

The accepted new words and phrases include:

BROKEBACK: Describing a gay man, after the officially banned film, *Brokeback Mountain.* Realizing its potential societal impact, the GLM named "Brokeback" the top HollyWord of the year it debuted.

EIGHT HONORS AND EIGHT DISGRACES: Reflecting desirable ethics, integrity, and what to avoid.

ERA OF SEVEN: The new era in Chinese economic history when the value of the official Chinese currency, the yuan, was set at seven to the dollar.

GRAY SKILLS: Career-enhancing skills such as drinking, singing karaoke, and card playing.

HOUSE SLAVES: People who bought a bigger house than they can afford, and so are bound to it.

MISTRESS EXPERTS: Nouveau riche businessmen who have established "second wives."

DINKs WITH PETS: (double income, no kids) but with pets.

SEMI-HONEY COUPLE: Couples that live far apart for economic reasons yet still maintain their relationship.

SMILING BEIJING: Intended to encourage a pleasant reception to guests who visit Beijing.

THREE-HANDED ILLNESS: Debilitating hand injuries due to the pulling of slot machines, sending text messages on cell phones, or playing video games.

The 2005 version of the *Contemporary Chinese Dictionary* added far more words (about 6,000) and deleted about 2,500 words considered to be outdated.

This differs from the practice of unabridged English dictionaries, where words are never dropped because they appear in the literature of the day. These English terms will still be referenced in print, the electronic media and the Internet although they may no longer be heard in contemporary speech.

Hindi + English = Hinglish

Of the various lishes in the world, the oldest and perhaps most venerable (if venerable is an appropriate word to describe a lish), is Hinglish (Hindi + English). This patois is spoken on the Indian Subcontinent—and increasingly across Southeast Asia. It's been called the Queen's Hinglish, and for good reason: it's probably been around since the first trader stepped off the ships of the British East India Company in the early 1600s. As the population of India and the surrounding region exploded over the past centuries, increasing numbers of its residents began assimilating English into their language. Now, China may have 250 million people *learning* English, but the Subcontinent has some 250 million people *speaking* English.

You can hear this phenomenon for yourself by dialing the customer service number for any of the world's largest corporations. I'm in the habit of asking customer service reps where I am calling. Most are instructed to say something like, "You are calling the customer service department of the Galactic Widget Corporation, which I might add has been voted the number one service experience by the good people of the Seychelles for the eighty-first year in a row." Though I am thinking, *The Seychelles? Eighty-one years? Was customer service even invented eighty years ago?* I say, "Where are you located physically?" to which the reply comes, "Mumbai" or "Chennai" or "Bangalore." India has literally turned its English-speaking ability, a once-embarrassing legacy of its colonial past, into a multibillion-dollar competitive advantage.

So what happens when you have hundreds of thousands of your

brightest students and employees (er, associates) speaking English on the phone and Hindi off-line? Hinglish!

Here are a few examples of Hinglish, which can also contain Urdu and Punjabi roots:

BADMASH: Naughty

CUDDIES: Underwear

FUNDOO: Cool (now also used in the United Kingdom and one of GLM's top Ten Global YouthSpeak Words for 2007)

GLASSY: In need of a drink

INNIT: Isn't it true?

PROPONE: The opposite of postpone—to move up a meeting or event

UNI: University (specific college unspecified)

STEPNEY: Literally a *spare tire*, an unnecessary addition, such as an unwelcome third person on a date.

TIMEPASS: Something done to pass the time

YOOFSPEAK: The patois spoken by youth (one of the Top Ten Global YouthSpeak Words for 2006)

Ketchup, Anyone? *Did you ever wonder why the word* ketchup *is spelled* ketchup *or* catsup *or even* catchup? *It's because* ketchup *derives from the Malaysian* kechap, *from the Chinese* ke-tsiap *(marinated vegetable sauce). In Malaysia, ketchup is more likely to be an eggplant-based sauce of which tomato ketchup is but one variety. Eggplant ketchup, anyone?*

Spanish + English = Spanglish

The combination of Spanish and English—Spanglish—has been going on since the days of John Cabot and the Conquistadors, but only recently has it reached a broader audience, as more and more Spanish speakers continue to emmigrate to the United States In the past, Spanglish was primarily confined to four distinct areas in this nation: Texas (historically a part of New Spain and Mexico), Southern California (because of the influx of Mexicans and South Americans), Miami (from Cuba and Latin America), and New York (courtesy of Puerto Rican, Latin America and the Caribbean nations). Recently, the Spanglish migration has entered the Heartland (from Des Moines to Minneapolis), the North, and the South. This expansion means that ever greater numbers of Spanglish words are certain to enter the mainstream.

We've all been witness to a rude English-speaking American with scant knowledge of Spanish (or any Romance language, for that matter) trying to convince a sales clerk that he wants to "purchase-o the Jello-O for dessert-o." But in fact, Spanglish is much more creative than that, actually mixing or melding words from the two languages, and sometimes even reimagining the words in completely differing ways.

Here are some Spanglish terms and their definitions:

> **Amigoization:** Increasing Mexican influence in California and the rest of the American Southwest
>
> **Backupear:** Backing up the car.
>
> **Changear:** To change
>
> **Chopin:** Shopping
>
> **Depurador:** Someone who debugs (makes pure) computer software

ENGLANOL: A Spanglish variation for Spanglish

ENJOYAR: To enjoy or like.

FLIPAR: To flip

FLONQUE: Flunk a test.

JANGUEAR: To hang out

LIBERIA: The library (not the country).

EL MACHINO: A machine (typically taco-making machines in the US)

MARQUETA: Grocery store, supermarket.

MENÚ DESPLEGABLE: Pop-up menu

NO PROBLEM-O: Mock Spanglish for "no worries"

PREGNEDA: Pregnant

RUFO: Roof of a building

SURFEAR LA INTERNET: Surf the Internet

SUPERMERCADO: supermarket

TEX-MEX: Spanglish bordering the Rio Grande (or Rio Brave)

TROCA: Pickup truck

YONQUE: Useless material, junk

Examples of Other Lishes (and One Lais):

LISH	MEANING	MY FAVORITE
Czechlish	Czech and English	Under-her-laundry (panties)
Denglish	Deutsch and English	Beamer (video projector)
Finglish	Finnish and English	Noobie (a rookie or beginner)
Franglais	French and English	Logiciel (software)
Manglish	Malaysian English	Outstation (going out of town)
Namlish	Nambian and English	. . . and what what (et cetera)
Poglish	Polish and English	Thanks for the mountain (thanks in advance)
Portinglês	Portuguese and English	Inicializar (to boot up or initialize)
Singlish	Singapore English	Act blur (feign confusion)
Swenglish	Swedish and English	Briefa (to brief someone)
Yinglish	Yiddish and English	Bulbenik (one who misses his cue; literally from *potato*)

How are all of these lishes going to impact the English language? It's undeniable that they've all had an influence, and their growing usage contributes great numbers of new words to the lexicon every year. But will English someday fracture into separate lishes like Latin devolving into the Romance languages? Throughout the history of the United States, the English language has taken on each new contender language (beginning with German at the time of the Revolutionary War), engulfed it, taken from it what it pleased, and moved on. Globally, this is a different question. I discuss the possible future scenarios for the English language at the end of this book.

The US–UK Divide: American English vs. British English

Winston Churchill famously observed that the American and British relationship was that of two peoples "divided by a common language." I remember some time ago, I was attending a lecture at the Harvard-Smithsonian Center for Astrophysics, located on a small hill north of Radcliffe Yard in Cambridge. The lecture delivered by a British astrophysicist was about various elements and their relative abundance in the solar system and beyond. Of course, he pronounced *iron* "i-ron," as opposed to the American "i-urn," and *schedule* with the first syllable pronounced as shed as opposed to the more common skej. That was no surprise. However, I was surprised to see *aluminum* pronounced as if ending "ium" rather than the more familiar "um." Later, when I was looking up the etymology, I was surprised to see that the element actually had two variations in spelling: *aluminum* and *aluminium*. (This variation occurs because the light, ductile metallic element, the most abundant found on earth, is derived from alumin(a) with the additional *i/um* suffix.) This instance put me on the lookout for the more exotic differences between Old World and New World English. Here are some of the examples that I've tracked over the years.

US vs UK

bangs vs. fringe

childish thinking vs. nappy-headed

counterclockwise vs. anticlockwise
(actually *widdershins*)

crosswalk vs. zebra crossing

diaper vs. nappy

drunk driving vs. drink driving

eggplant vs. aubergine

fanny pack vs. bumbag

highway, Interstate, expressway or freeway vs. motorway

John Q. Public vs. Joe Public

line vs. queue

math vs. maths

pacifier vs. dummy (the baby "soother," not a peacemaker).

plastic wrap vs. cling film

potato chips or chips vs. crisps

semi or 16-wheeler or tractor-trailer vs. articulated lorry

shopping cart vs. shopping trolley

stroller vs. pushchair

tempest in a teapot vs. storm in a teacup

tic-tac-toe vs. naughts and crosses

trash/garbage can vs. dustbin

truck stop vs. transport café

unlisted vs. ex-directory

zucchini vs. courgette

z vs. zed

Widdershins

Widdershins, literally "against the sun," contains within itself a brief history of the role of time in Western civilization. Originally, time was governed by the Sun (and the Moon and stars). Every day, the Sun rose in the East and set in the West. This was the natural order of things. Things moved from East to West, the same motion as the sun (facing North, from right to left, this came to be called *sunwise*). Later, when mechanical clocks were first invented in the thirteenth century, their hour and minute hands were constructed to move in a *sunwise* direction. This direction later became known as *clockwise*. When the hands of the clock or anything else moved in the opposite direction, this became known as *counterclockwise*.

CHAPTER FIVE

The Cutting Edge
How Culture Changes the Way We Communicate

Every year the amount of recorded history (or herstory, if you prefer) doubles. And this doubling of information continues to quicken:
within a few years, it will occur every month, every week, every day,
every hour, every minute, and then every second. So the question is:
How do we adapt to this mind-boggling acceleration in the accumulation of information?

One way is to recognize that this accumulation is of information,
and not knowledge. Another is to recognize that as it is processed
into knowledge, it will probably be output in Global English. The
last time Western civilization encountered such a rapid increase in
the accumulation of knowledge was during what we now call the
Renaissance, beginning with the invention of movable type. What's
interesting here is that the people of the Renaissance (from the
French for "rebirth") did not consider themselves to be living in an
era of rebirth—they were too busy living it. (It was not until the
nineteenth century that Matthew Arnold came up with the now familiar appellation, although he Anglicized it as *Renascence*.) It is very
likely that we, too, are living in a new type of "renaissance," with our

rapid expansion of knowledge possibly changing the very fabric of civilization as we now know it—without knowing it.

Culture is much more than a sum total of this information and/or knowledge; rather, it is "the totality of socially transmitted behavior patterns, arts, beliefs, institutions, and all other products of human work and thought," as yourDictionary.com defines it. Culture is primarily transferred through the spoken language and through exposition, the written form of the spoken language. (Of course, there are other means of transmitting cultural knowledge, such as a "griot" reciting generational histories, or the "guipas" of the Peruvian Incas who recorded their history on knotted ropes.) In today's culture, the youth of the world are often the progenitors of the evolution of language in general, and in Global English in particular. Their verbal variations and affectations often sweep the world of Global English and the Internet in a matter of days.

This chapter will help you understand how contemporary culture changes the manner in which we communicate.

TOP U.S. YOUTHSPEAK WORDS

Recently, we've had to expand our definition of youthSpeak (or yoofSpeak, as it's called in the Pan-Asian arena) to include emoticons and SMS (or text messages) in our list of catchphrases. These additions signal yet another fascinating trend in the rise of Global English among the world's youth.

The words spoken by American youth will be the words spoken by the world's youth thirty-six months hence. Study the following list and you won't get caught using outdated lingo.

A'IGHT: All right. As in, "That girl is nice, she's a'ight."

BANK: Has lots of flow (see also *flow*)

BIZZNIZZLE: Business. As in "None of your bizznizzle!" Part of the Snoop Dogg/Sean John–inspired lexicon.

BLING: Originally *bling-bling*, the sounds of jewelry (preferably diamonds and gold) clinking together, *bling* now refers to any expensive or ostentatious jewelry.

CHILLIN': Relaxing, especially with friends.

COOL: Still a cool word, even after 100 years.

CRUNK: A Southern variation of hip-hop music. Also means "fun" or "amped."

DOPE: (1) Excellent, cool, tight, or phat. As in, "That's totally dope!" (2) Fine, good.

FLOW: Money. Originally from "cash flow" (see also *bank*).

FO' SHIZZLE: Variation of "for sure," popularized by the hip-hop community.

FRESH: Smooth, great-looking.

GIVE IT UP! Replaces the square "Please give a round of applause for . . ."

HELLA: An intensive: *hella* tight or *hella* phat.

HOTTIE: Object of affection, either personally or in the cultural milieu.

MAD: A lot, as in, "She has mad money."

PEACE (or *peace out*): "See you later."

PHAT: Way cool, as in "rolling phat."

PIMPIN: Good with women (also *playa*).

POPPINS: Perfect, from "Mary Poppins is perfect in every way."

PROPER: Right, correct; a recycled Britishism.

PROPS: Respect or credit. As in, "He gets mad props!" Can also be used in place of *kudos, cheers* or *congratulations.*

RICE ROCKETS: Tricked out Japanese compact cars, as opposed to American "muscle" cars.

SHUT UP! Really?

SICK: Hella cool!

SIDE SHOW: The temporary cordoning off of a freeway, done to perform outrageous car stunts in tricked-out rice rockets.

SNAG: Sensitive New-Age Guy.

STOG: Cigarette, short for "stogie."

SWEATIN': Irritating, bugging. As in, "He's really sweatin' me!"

TIGHT: Cool.

TRICKED OUT: Souped-up.

WASSUP? WHAT UP? and **S'UP?** Popular variations of "What's up?" or "What's going on?"

WORD: That's good, that's OK, or that's right.

Bonus Youthspeak Phenomenon of Note:

UP TALKING: Ending all sentences with a rising or upward inflection, as if asking a question.

THE TOP 10 GLOBAL YOUTHSPEAK WORDS

Not as avant-garde as America's but perhaps more colorful, the following words are popular among the rest of the world's youth.

1. *YoofSpeak* (Pan Asia): YouthSpeak.

2. *Ballin'*: Doing well; fine; as in, "He's really ballin' now."

3. *Stick Ice* (China): Popsicle or ice-cream cone.

4. *Ya-ya papaya* (Singapore): Snooty person

5. *Get up one's nose* (UK): Irritates. As in, "He gets up my nose!"

6. *Yobbo* (Australia/UK): An unrefined or loutish youth. (Back slang.)

7. *Mang:* Variation of man from hip-hop. As in, "S'up, mang?"

8. *Brill!* (UK): The shortened form of "brilliant"

9. *Fully* (Australia): Extremely. As in, "fully sick."

10. *Fundoo* (India/UK): Cool

Words on the Go: Text Messaging, Instant Messaging, and Our New Electronic Language

Texting is now one of the newest, and the most popular, ways to communicate around the world. As I write these words, about a billion text messages (formally known as SMS messages, for short message service) are sent every day. And, as you have probably surmised, this number is growing rapidly. So important are text messages and instant messaging to the business world, they are now covered by regulatory and compliance initiatives from federal governments worldwide. Here are a few examples of text message-speak:

OMG: Oh. My. God.

LMAO: Laughed my ass off.

II: Siigniifiies the text messaging style of doubliing the letter ii wherever iit iis found. Considered to be preppy.

1: A sign-off, from the U2 song "One Love."

9: Parent is watching.

99: Parent is no longer watching.

ADIP: Another day in paradise.

BBB: Boring beyond belief.

IMO or **IMHO:** In my opinion or in my humble opinion.

NMJCHAY: Not much, just chillin', how about you?

SSEWBA: Some day soon, everything will be acronyms. (OK, I made that one up.)

EMOTICONS

Informally called *smileys* because the earliest emoticons consisted of the smiley face ☺ (a pre-Internet emoticon) and variations thereof, emoticons constitute an entirely new way of representing words in exposition. However, this form of exposition is not putting pen to paper but rather thumb or finger to LCD or keypads of various electronic handheld devices. Here are some notable emoticons you might encounter:

Abraham Lincoln: =|:-)=

Angel: 0:-)

Bad hair day: =:-)

Child's smile: :)

Confused: %)

Drunk: : #)

Foot in mouth: :-!

Frowning: (:-(

Geek or nerd (from "propeller head"): X:-)

Hair Line, glasses, moustache, and goatee: /8^{~<

Hung over: %*@:-(

Keep a secret: :-# (i.e., "My lips are sealed.")

Mickey Mouse: 8(:-)

A nerd: 8-)

New haircut: @:-}

Omigod: 8-O

Priest: +:-)

Ronald Reagan: 7:^]

Toupee alert: {(:-)

The emoticon representing a kitty: =^..^=

The smiley that started it all: :-)
(1982—originally called a "joke marker")

Top Global Musical Trends and Words

Words from music permeate Global English. Some terms that have come to global recognition include *rock* (or rock 'n' roll), *jazz*, and *rap* or *hip-hop*. Words such as *bling* (originally *bling-bling*, an onomatopoeic term for the sound of diamonds clinking together) quickly jump from lyrics to lifestyle, and eventually enter the common lexicon. Here are some more musical terms that seem to be following the same path:

> AFROPOP: Pop music from the African continent characterized by distinctive rhythms, indigenous roots, cross-cultural influences and unique combinations of rural and urban styles. These include:

> | | | |
> |---|---|---|
> | Apala | Kwaito | Raï |
> | Bikutsi | Kwela | Sakara |
> | Isicathamiya | Makossa | Soukous |
> | Jit | Mbube | Taarab |
> | Jùjú | | |

> ANIME MUSIC VIDEO (AMV): Anime music videos are constructed of clips of anime cartoons featuring characters with large eyes, exaggerated hair, and out-of-proportion limbs.

> HIGH SCHOOL MUSICAL: The global phenomenon of yet another version of Romeo and Juliet, with star-crossed teen lovers from different cliques in this version. The musical is taking dozens of shapes in scores of countries, all in English, of course, except for the Hindi version.

HIP-HOP CULTURE: The lifestyle surrounding the hip-hop movement typically characterized by singing, breakdancing, DJs, emceeing, and graffiti art. A now-global phenomenon, though hip-hop music has largely lost its most favored status to gangsta rap.

WORLD MUSIC: Also referred to as "folk," "roots" or "traditional" music, including indigenous music and songs from around the world. Western music is generally excluded with the rare exception of certain folk traditions such as Celtic music.

MBUBE: A genre of South African a capella singing named after a song composed by Solomon Linda (related to *isicathamiya*).

MP3: Not a recently unmasked British black ops agency, but rather one of many (though perhaps most popular) formats for playing music on electronic and portable musical MP3 devices.

PODCAST: Shortened form of iPod broadcast, a podcast is a digital media file distributed over the Internet using syndication feeds for playback on computers of portable media.

REGGAETON (pronounced *reggae-TONE*): Part Latin, part hip-hop, with liberal helpings of dancehall and Caribbean music thrown in for good measure. Several Reggaeton radio staples this year made their way into widespread public consciousness.

EMO: A music style often likened to re-cycled punk. Also a subculture, the emo lifestyle, extending into clothing (tight pants and sweatshirts), horned-rim glasses, and often melancholy temperaments.

BAILE (pronounced *bye-lay*) FUNK: Brazilian dance music that has gained popularity worldwide, championed by such trend-setters as Norman Cook in the UK, and Philadelphia DJ Diplo.

BAND AID, LIVE AID, and LIVE 8: A series of rock concert benefits staged to help alleviate third-world poverty, AIDS, and to encourage the G-9 to foster debt relief to impoverished nations.

BITTORRENT: A method of distributing large amounts of data through peer-to-peer file sharing. In a very complex manner, computers find other computers to share random bits of data that are reassembled into music or video files, utilizing swarms, peers and torrents.

CRUNK: A Southern variation of hip-hop music; also a global YouthSpeak word meaning fun or amped (itself a word borrowed from electronic music).

THE: The definite pronoun is definitely *in* in rock music, from The Strokes to The Vines to The Hives to The The.

THROAT SINGING: A Central-Asian singing style where harmonic resonances are used to create a melody. Also known as *overtone singing*.

RINGTONES: Not a new trend, but certainly an accelerating one. Custom ringtones are now heard from Tuvalu to Timbuktu.

!!!: Symbolizes the rise of bands that give themselves unpronounceable names consisting or letters or orthographic symbols, following the lead of the erstwhile "singer formerly known as Prince," who created his very own symbol.

(): Albums with symbols as names. This album by Sigur Rós contains a songbook of 12 blank pages.

Fashionistas and the Global Fashion Industry

The trillion-dollar global fashion industry is unlike any other. By its very definition, the word *fashion* derives from the Middle English *facioun*, and ultimately from the past participle of the Latin *facere*, "to make [or] do." (Of course, if you trace the word *fashion* back to the Proto-Indo-European, you can see that it also relates to *doom*, *feckless*, and *sacrifice*.) Now, the word *do* is one of the most basic words in any language because it describes one of the key constituents of the human condition: *doing* something, which encompasses all human activities from baking bread to pondering infinity to *doing* absolutely nothing.

So fashion is nothing special until you get to the most prevalent definition referring to the typical manner of dress in a society, culture, subculture, or time period, such as in Roman Times, the Renaissance, China of the Sung Dynasty, the antebellum American South, the Court of the Sun King, or, even, London in the 1960s or the contemporary showgirl culture of Las Vegas.

Fashion fascinates. It tells us something about ourselves and our times. Now, think about clothing and our times. Think about what you wear. There are many distinctions between what we are now wearing (fashionable or not) and what people wore, say, a hundred or even fifty years ago. And I am not thinking here of the wonder fabrics of nylon, rayon, spandex, and the lot. A principle distinction is the use of clothing for messaging, which is certainly an innovative use of exposition and language.

Next time you venture outside your home, take a quick look at the people about you. How many are wearing clothing that bears words? Even complete thoughts or sentences, and once in a great while, a paragraph or two? We've all been well acclimated by this phenomenon and don't give it a second thought, though words are frequently inscribed on hats, jackets, blouses, shirts, and skirts, even undergarments.

Advertising, of course, plays a part in this. Even designers of haute couture cannot resist embedding their initials into their couture designs. I remember reading in the early '80s that Blaise Cendrars, the Swiss-French iconoclastic writer of the early part of the last century, included "advertising" in his "Ten Wonders of the Modern World." (His most famous poem was never published, neither written down, nor even spoken aloud. When he completed what he considered to be his greatest novel, he left it hidden in a trunk in an attic of an unnamed house in Brazil. It has never been found.)

The word *fashion* is also often used in relation to *vogue*, *style*, and *mode*. *Style* is the *mode* of dress *en vogue* for what used to be called "polite society." The term *vogue* usually implies a fashion flash, or short-lived phenomenon, such as the ultra-wide collars on men's shirts that were *en vogue* during the disco era (1977–80).

The old proverb that words, actually reckless words, pierce as a sword, was certainly in my mind as I read an article in *The Times of India* that claimed the whole of the Indian fashion industry was abuzz about a recent Global Language Monitor analysis of the top fashion capitals of the world. Our analysis, of course, was based on the frequency, contextual usage, and the number of appearances of fashion-capital related words and phrases in the global media, the Internet, and throughout the blogosphere. The controversy lay in the fact that the analysis ranked Mumbai (the former Bombay) ahead of Delhi, the traditional seat of Indian fashion. The "debate" as *The Times of India* captures it, concerns the fact that although Delhi "has the government backing, the technical know how . . . and 80% of

India's fashion designers"—Mumbai made it into the Top 20 "whereas there was no mention of Delhi."

The debate evidently raged for some time among Delhi "fashion week" promoters, government agencies, the designers themselves, and various "fashionistas," while Mumbai designers, movie moguls, and anyone remotely involved could scarcely contain their glee.

The reason, of course, was, is, and will continue to be, Bollywood as in Hollywood. For Mumbai is the capital of the Subcontinent's massive movie-making machine. And although Delhi may, indeed, be the capital of the Indian fashion industry, where Indian fashion influences the globe, those influences will spring from Mumbai. Words, indeed, pierce like a sword or, perhaps, in this case, like a pair of pinking shears.

There were also debates about the Sydney vs. Melbourne rankings: Sydney outdistanced Melbourne, but Melbourne was gaining momentum in the global media. And then there was Cracow (No. 25) vs. Chicago (unranked). Chicago would do fairly well on the global rankings but not emerge into the Top 25, while Cracow is now regarded as the center of Neo-Bohemian influence on the Continent. Chicago has the largest concentration of Poles in the United States, ranking second globally only to Warsaw.

A Ranking of the Global Fashion Capitals of 2007

Topping the list for the 2007 fashion season were New York, Rome, Paris, London, Milan, Tokyo, Los Angeles, Hong Kong, Las Vegas, and Singapore. Breaking into the Top 25 were Berlin (No. 11), Shanghai (No. 14), Moscow (No. 16), and Dubai (No. 24). Other notable rankings included Shanghai at No. 14, Sydney and Melbourne at Nos. 12 and 15 respectively, and the Fashion Quartet of South America: Santiago, Rio de Janeiro, São Paulo, and Buenos Aires. No. 25 was Cracow, making the ranking because of its emerging status as center of neo-Bohemian influence.

The ranking was surprising in a number of ways, most of which relate to the changing nature of the global fashion industry. Cities that recently would have been considered fashion backwaters—or worse, are now emerging as significant regional hubs.

Of course, the ranking was based upon the Predictive Quantities Indicator that I mentioned earlier.

1. New York—Far and away No. 1 by every index

2. Rome—Beats out Paris, London and Milan

3. Paris—Hearbeat of the fashion world

4. London—Pulsing with creative energy

5. Milan—Perennial contender for No. 1

6. Tokyo—Gaining global influence

7. Los Angeles—Will Posh Spice impact ranking? :-)

8. Hong Kong—No. 1 in South Asia

9. Las Vegas—Emerging as vibrant fashion center

10. Singapore—Strong regional hub

11. Berlin—Big fashion push and it's working

12. Sydney—Oz scores two in the Top 20

13. Barcelona—Regional center grows in stature

14. Shanghai—China breaks into the big time

15. Melbourne—Greater momentum than Sydney

16. Moscow—Lenin would not be amused

17. Bangkok—Realizing its dream

18. Mumbai—Indian fashion influences globe

19. Santiago—Major strides for a proud nation

20. Rio de Janeiro—More than Carnivale and Ipanema

21. São Paulo—Money and fashion *do* mix

22. Buenos Aires—Seat of classic beauty returns

23. Johannesburg—Jo-burg narrowly outdistances rival Cape Town

24. Dubai—Dubai? Yes, Dubai.

25. Crakow—Neo-Bohemia thrives

In the special category for swimwear, Miami took top honors for its transformation from the capital of the Caribbean Basin, to the whole of Latin America, and finally the world.

SOME FASHION JARGON

The perfect blend of the runways of Paris, Milan, and New York, with a heavy admixture of Hollywood stars, and the five-hundred-channel world of television with its insatiable need for "content," has made the world of fashion more accessible (and more popular) than ever. Of course, this fact has made an impact upon Global English. The following list is but a sampling of how the fashion industry has impacted Global English.

> BLACK IS THE NEW . . . : Basic black is the traditional haute couture color; every season new colors are introduced, some of which might sweep through the fashion world as "the new black." This has become a formulaic expression, "A is the new B," applied far afield of the world of fashion, such as "age fifty is the new forty" or "random is the new order."

SOURCING: Determining the "source" from which various textiles can be acquired; often used in a global sense.

DRESSY CASUAL: Casual elegance; one of the many definitions of casual dress is various situations that include:

Active Casual	Rugged Casual
Business Casual	Smart Casual
Casual Casual	Sporty Casual
Dressy casual	

FASHION VICTIM: Applied to those who overstep the bounds of the current style, either by going to extremes or unknowingly committing a fashion "faux pas."

FASHION FAUX PAS: Literally a false step; dressing inappropriately without being aware of it.

SIZE-ZERO: The smallest size in women's clothing; an often destructive goal for young women and girls.

FASHIONISTA: A fashion enthusiast, often with a negative connotation.

REGENERATED FIBER: Fibers made from natural materials, such as rayon or lyocell, which are made from wood pulp (cellulose).

FASHION MONGER: A serious student of fashion; often used pejoratively.

NUBBLES: Any type of wool or yarn that adds texture because of its nubs or nubbiness.

FASHION TRIBE: Persons who follow a particular fashion with a tribe-like mindset; examples include emo, hip-hop or goth.

WARP AND WEFT KNITS: In warp knits, the yarn runs lengthwise; in weft knits, yarns interlock across the fabric.

SOME TIMELESS FASHION TERMINOLOGY

ATELIER: A studio or workroom where high-fashion garments are made (also known as a designer's studio).

BIAS: A line going diagonally across the grain of fabric.

BUYER: The person who buys the apparel for department stores (sometimes also known as the purchaser).

CHIC: Elegant and fashionable.

COUTURE: High-end clothing that designers create for an exclusive market of individual customers and exclusive boutiques, made to each customer's measurements.

COUTURIER: The designers who present a collection each season aimed at rich private customers. Originally the French word for "dressmaker."

HAUTE: High (as in *haute couture*), what is stylish at the moment.

MOTIF: A recurring element, such as decorative stitching, colors, or fabric choices, which a designer inserts into an item of clothing, or throughout an entire collection.

PRÊT-À-PORTER: Ready-to-wear, a range of clothing that is mass produced. This is what most of us wear.

RAG TRADE: The apparel industry: makers and sellers of fashionable clothing.

TEXTILE: Fabric or cloth, made by any number of techniques such as weaving, knitting, or plaiting.

TOILE: A muslin or calico garment, made up to show how a design will look before cutting the actual fabric.

VINTAGE: Used clothing from an earlier time or of an earlier style, or new clothing that just *appears* to be older.

CHAPTER SIX

Working Nine to Five

How Corporate Culture Contributes to the Public Vocabulary

CorporateSpeak

Amy Joyce, the workplace columnist from the *Washington Post*, called me one afternoon to ask me what I thought of the words used to describe the dismissal of a key administration official, who said he was leaving his job "to spend more time with his family." As our discussion progressed, I mentioned that I had been a senior executive for communications and marketing at three or four Fortune

> **Starting from Ground Zero** *This is CorporateSpeak in its most basic form. In actuality, "ground zero" defines the epicenter of a nuclear explosion. When your boss tells your team that you have to "start from ground zero," I am quite sure he is not instructing you to restart the task from a mile-deep, 1,000,000°F radioactive pit. (After 9/11, use of the term in this manner has become even more problematic.)*

500 corporations (depending how you count them: pre- or postacquisition), as well as at a series of Silicon Valley start-ups, restarts, and upstarts. I wondered aloud, "Have you ever heard of someone taking a job to spend *less time* with his or her family?" She replied, "Never!" Anyone who follows corporate politics knows what "leaving to spend more time with my family" and "leaving to pursue other options" really means. It means they have been summarily fired.

Amy Joyce and I then went on to talk about the existence of CorporateSpeak (CS), which, if not a separate dialect, certainly constitutes a sort of patois, mastered by tens of thousands of $CxOs$ (see sidebar, page 112) and their like (or ilk, if you prefer). There are 6,920 distinct human dialects on this planet. (And this does not include Visual Basic, ADA, or C++, or any of the various pidgin strains that flourish in the vicinity of Tech Square in Cambridge or off "the 101" in Silicon Valley.) But unlike all of them, CorporateSpeak follows a precise set of rules that have little to do with syntax, semantics, and the like. Rather, the rules of CorporateSpeak could better be viewed as rules of engagement. For with CorporateSpeak, as with everything else on the corporate battlefield, any weakness that one unwittingly exposes will be swiftly exploited by your competition (be they across the hall or around the globe).

Granted, not every manager strives to be perceived as educated, or even intelligent. In some circles it's actually countercultural to be viewed as such. You definitely do not want to be branded as an intellectual (CorporateSpeak for "no guts") or a dreamer (CorporateSpeak for "no glory").

But in today's global marketplace, you also may not want to present yourself as if English were your second language. Especially when your competitor from China, the Subcontinent, or South Miami, for that matter, might easily best you in *your* native tongue.

And this is where CorporateSpeak comes in: helping the brilliant corporate strategist, the clever marketing tactician, the productive product manager, the inscrutable yet inventive engineer, and the finance guru communicate their purposeful, even lofty visions in simple and intelligible language. More simply put, to use CS is to successfully transport ideas from one cranium to another.

Of course, the ability to communicate effectively enough to inspire others is rarely a prerequisite for entrance to, nor is it readily taught in, most business schools. There, it is widely assumed that you picked it up at the commencement ceremony along with your baccalaureate degree. Of course, this knowledge was not readily available in college, since it was widely assumed that it was delivered to you along with your high school diploma, the week after the senior prom. Of course, this knowledge was not readily available in high school, since . . . well, you get the idea.

More to the point—you can't acquire this knowledge through a skillful (if mind-numbing) reading of, say, *Freakonomics*, *In Search of Excellence*, *Crossing the Chasm*, or even the most current issue of *HBR*.

CxO

CxOs are part of title inflation. At one time you just had a president of a company. But now, if the company is "public," that is, owned by stakeholders (shareholders) in a corporation, there is also a chairperson or even "chair" (chairman) of that corporation. How to know who is actually running the company? The chief executive officer (CEO), of course.

Corporations now routinely have chief *operating* officers, chief *information* officers, chief *strategic* officers, and chief *marketing* officers, among others. And yourDictionary.com even had a chief *linguistic* officer. (Disclaimer: My title at the Global Language Monitor is president and chief word analyst.)

Hence, the term CxO, the *x* standing for the unknown in the corporate equation.

The Letter X

Since we're on the subject of the letter *x*, what do you think the *x* stands for in the Christmas variation, Xmas? Rather than taking "Christ out of Christmas," as some suppose, it is actually using one of the most ancient (and sacred) symbols of the Christ, a shortened form of the chi (*x*), the first Greek letter of the honorific.

It's much more subtle than that, though it *is* largely a matter of executive presence or style.

Of course, one of the many benefits of a classical (if politically incorrect) education is the ability to express complex ideas in a meaningful yet simple manner. And when employed by talented businesspeople, this can even be achieved in expository Corporate-Speak, which is to say the written form of the spoken language.

A FEW RULES FOR CORPORATESPEAK

> ► Never use Latinisms—e.g., i.e., etc.—when English will suffice (unless, of course, their use will confuse your competition in ways advantageous to you).
>
> By the way, *i.e.* is Latin for *id est*, which means simply "it is," while *e.g.* is Latin for *exempli gratia*, which means "by way of example."
>
> Think in English and the phrases will automatically sort themselves out. Also, remember that *i.e.* refers to a definitive list, whereas *e.g.* refers to a finite example of a much larger list.

➤ **Strive for simplicity.**

Three words on simplicity: Less is more. Put another way: The more complex the ideas, the simpler the style.

The greatest ideas are invariably conveyed in the simplest, most precise, most elegant manner. Complex structures are ultimately built of simple building blocks, right?

➤ *Non multiplicanda entia sine necessitate.*

This phrase, known as Occam's Razor, is actually the basis of civilization as we know it, since it's the precursor of the scientific method. It translates as "Do not multiply things beyond necessity," which seems like a pretty good way of looking at most things in life. William of Occam (1285–1349), known in his time as the Invincible Doctor, was one of the first to maintain that reason and logic were insufficient without empirical evidence. He saw that in logic, it is best to avoid unnecessary extrapolations. In fact, the simplest, most elegant explanation is usually the best one.

➤ **Remember that your performance is always judged on your most recent success (or failure). And in fast-moving fields, victory in one quarter can be looked upon as a definitive defeat or even disaster in the next.**

The Romans had a phrase for this, *sic transit gloria mundi*, literally "Thus passes the glory of the world." Who was the Bill Gates of Rome? Someone had to mastermind all the advance technology of their time, in this case civil engineering. Who controlled all the IP, or intellectual property, for building those aqueducts and roads, many of which are still in use in the twenty-first century? Who built the Colosseum, the

Spin, the Problem Thereof

Spin is a rather curious word. Heads spin. Tops spin. Even the Earth spins (rather than rotates). But when we speak of spin, of course, we are not referring to the intrinsic angular momentum of a subatomic particle, but rather to an unbridled (and often unsubtle) attempt to shade or sway public attitude and/or opinion.

Spin is not precisely the same thing as hype (see *hyperbole*, from the Latin *hyperbole*, from the Greek *hyperballein*, "to throw excessively"), but *hype*'s as good a place as any to start when addressing this rather arcane subject.

According to the established rules of hype, you must convolute your communications by using *utilize* instead of utilizing *use*, or *allows to* when *lets* would actually make more sense. This is the rarely stated but often practiced "more is more" principle. I claim this as my own.

Years ago when I was working on a Japanese computer workstation (an ideographic word processor, to be precise), I learned that there are only 40,000 commonly used kanji ideograms, or words, in Japanese. At that time, you couldn't just type an ideogram, you had to assemble them from a keyboard of some 200 keys. A good typist could produce a dozen or so ideograms per minute, as compared to more than 100 words in English.

The Japanese solved the problem by creating the Japanese Industrial Interchange Code (JIIC). This limited most business and government correspondence to some 2,000 ideograms. They had no choice but to uphold the "less is more" axiom.

Of course, in English, with our million words, we have the opposite problem, trying to decide which among this multitude to utilize, er, use. Hence, our tendency to err on the side of "more is more."

Forum, and the rest of the infrastructure of the nation? Who was Rome's Donald Trump? *Sic transit gloria mundi.* Indeed.

TOP CORPORATESPEAK

CREATIVE DESTRUCTION: The natural process by which new companies and technologies supplant their predecessors.

FIN DE BUBBLE: Similar to the fin de siècle period of pre-World War I Europe, where everyone knew things were headed in a bad direction but nevertheless remained optimistic about their circumstances.

GAMING: Softer, kinder, gentler word than gambling, now a multi-billion dollar source of global revenue for both the private and public sector.

CUSTOMER EXPERIENCE: Postmodernism for "Customer Service"; also, Chief Customer Experience Officer.

EFFORT: As in "We are efforting to resolve the glitch." Like "to concept" ("We are in the concepting stage"), this is another example of too much "verbing."

TO ENRON: A company publicly implodes from its own missteps and perceived greed.

FROTHY: A fresh or original idea.

RESONATE: Rather than "relate to," an idea now "resonates" with customers. Literally, the tendency of a system to oscillate at maximum amplitude at a certain frequency. Sample use: "Our customers really oscillate at maximum amplitude for our new product set!"

LOW-HANGING FRUIT: Easy-to-win sales; for example, "I want you all to go after the low-hanging fruit!"

OUTSOURCING: Sending the production of products and services "off-shore."

OUT-OF-THE-BOX EXPERIENCE: Contemporary re-phrasing of "Does Mikey like it?" Positive "out-of-the-box experience" truly "resonates" with the customer.

TRANSFORMATIVE TECHNOLOGIES: Technologies that change the "paradigm" of a business, such as 8-tracks yielding to cassettes and cassettes giving way to CDs or compact discs. (See "A new paradigm," page 118.)

Business English

A new phenomenon has recently appeared (or rather, it has recently been confirmed to exist by the global business community): Business English. Business English can best be defined as "English for professional purposes."

It is an acknowledged fact that to succeed in the twenty-first-century economy, which is interconnected, increasingly borderless, and 24/7/365, you must have a common means of discourse. Of course, this common language is a subset of Global English. Business English, which consists of perhaps two-thousand words, has become a prerequisite to conduct business on this planet of ours. Though it uses the English language, the words in its vocabulary are not necessarily simple or easy to understand. For example, in Business English we might say, "This paradigm shift has resulted directly from the e-quake." Say what?

The rise of Business English could, perhaps, be viewed as inversely proportional to the decline of the nation-state. (Few realize how recently the nation-state came into being. Three, maybe four hundred years ago?) The largest corporations now dwarf most nations in terms of Gross Domestic Product (GDP, the sum total of all the goods and services produced in a country in a calendar year).

Wal-Mart is approaching a half *trillion* dollars per year in what the Brits call "turnover." Turnover, in nation-state terms, is comparable to GDP. On the World Bank's list of national GDPs, Wal-Mart would rank ahead of 170 nations, reaching into the top 20. Fortunately, Wal-Mart has not yet raised a standing army.

Because of the potent combination of corporate culture and constitutional democracy, Americans grow up in a hypercompetitive, free-market economy in which business jargon creeps naturally into everyday conversation. Americans are always "pushing the envelope," or "crossing the chasm," or "introducing a new paradigm," although few know where these phrases originated.

> PUSHING THE ENVELOPE: Originally "pushing the edge of the envelope," from test pilot jargon as documented by Tom Wolfe in *The Right Stuff*. The "envelope" is the known performance limits of the plane that the pilot is testing. It was his job to push beyond those limits. (Prior to the popularization of this phrase, the "envelope" was better known as a set of boundary conditions in mathematics.)

> CROSSING THE CHASM: Originated by Geoffrey Moore in his 1991 book *Crossing the Chasm*. The central idea is that in the high-tech world, it is not the technological innovator who makes a product a success, but those who "cross the chasm" with their product and effectively deliver it to the pragmatists (who make up the "early majority" of mainstream buyers).

> A NEW PARADIGM: In Thomas Kuhn's *The Structure of Scientific Revolutions*, he defines a scientific paradigm as a way of seeing the world that prevails during differing time periods. For example, Copernicus's helio-

California Olive Growers Association Size Classifications

These just might be the folks who invented media "hype":

Large

Extra Large

Jumbo

Gigantic

Colossal

Super-Colossal

centric (Sun-centered) theory, which replaced the earlier Earth-centered dogma of Ptolemy that had held sway for the better part of two millennia, can be considered a paradigm. In the business world, a paradigm has come to mean any new plan that might provide a competitive edge.

Because CorporateSpeak and Business English are two of the principal drivers of the globalization of the language, they are particularly interesting as a subject of study and analysis. In the future, look for universities and business schools around the globe to begin offering Business English as a subject of serious study. It is already, without a doubt, a prerequisite to entering the global economy.

Words from Advertising

Blaise Cendrars was quite possibly on to something, at least where advertising—and words—are concerned. Advertising has long been decried as a bane for language, when in fact its steady creation of new words and phrases has been an absolute boon for language.

SOME INTERESTING WORDS AND PHRASES FROM THE WORLD OF ADVERTISING

COFFEE BREAK: Inspired by a promotional campaign in the late 1940s to get people to drink more coffee at scheduled breaks from work.

NYLON: a name coined by DuPont Corporation in the 1930s to echo the sounds of cotton and rayon. Nylon was created as "synthetic silk" to be used in the parachutes of World War II. However, it first became known as artificial silk stockings, thereafter called "ladies' nylons."

CHICAGOLAND: a now-forgotten auto dealer's slogan for yet another "Tri-state Area" or SMSA (Standard Metropolitan Statistical Area) captures the imagination and becomes a very useful appellation.

XEROX: From the branded and trademarked photocopying process (from the Greek *xero*, "dry"). Marketing 101 thinking calls for the strongest protection of trademarks. One reason, of course, is to protect against competition infringing upon your intellectual property. A secondary and oft-stated reason is to ensure that the trademarked word does not slip into everyday language, thus becoming a *word* devoid of any copyright protection. Example often cited: Xerox. Other common examples include Band-aids, Jell-O, and Kleenex.

From a Global English point of view, adding a word like Xerox to the language enriches it by describing a technical process never before accomplished, but also introduces an entirely new generation to classical Greek.

GOOGLE: A misspelling of the word *googol*, which was coined at the age of nine by Milton Sirotta, a nephew of the American mathematician Edward Kasner (1878–1955). *Googol* is defined as the number 100 followed by 100 zeroes.

Google's founders, Larry Page and Sergey Brin, apparently were unaware of the misspelling when they registered the company in 1998. In an apparent play on the original word, their corporate headquarters is informally known as the Googleplex. (See "Galaxies," page 135.)

This is what a googol looks like.
1,000,000,000,000, 000,000,000, 000,000,000, 000,000,000, 000,000,000, 000,000,000, 000,000,000, 000,000,000,000, 000,000, 000,000,000, 000,000,000

THINGS GO BETTER WITH COKE: As a child, this slogan made me think, "What exactly is a 'thing' and why do 'things' go better with a carbonated beverage"? YourDictionary.com defines a *thing* as:

n. 1. An entity, an idea, or a quality perceived, known, or thought to have its own existence. 2. a. The real or concrete substance of an entity. b. An entity existing in space and time. c. An inanimate object.

Now, if you go back to the Proto-Indo-European, you see that the word *thing* is "cognate" with or related to *think*, *thumb*, and *thingamabob*.

So one might ask what does Coke have to do with making inanimate objects go better? And once you think that one through, why exactly is Coke "the real inanimate object"? For that matter, why exactly does "Coke add life?"—*Life* being "the property or quality that distinguishes living organisms from dead organisms and inanimate matter."

GOT MILK? This is perhaps one of the most parodied advertising campaigns of all time. Originally launched by the California Milk Processor Board in 1993, to increase the consumption of milk, the emphasis on the word *got* is of great interest.

- ➤ Got Jesus?
- ➤ Got Sun?
- ➤ Got Sand?
- ➤ Got Snow?
- ➤ Got Kids?
- ➤ Got Game?
- ➤ Got Help?
- ➤ Got Life?
- ➤ Got Chocolate?
- ➤ Got Junk?

What exactly does the word *got* got that makes it work in so many ways?

Got is the past participle of the word *get*. *Get* is one of those words, like *set* and *go*, that have literally scores of meanings. When you go back to the Prot-Indo-European, you find that *get* is ultimately derived from *ghend* that originally meant "to take or to seize." Interestingly enough, derivatives from *ghend* include *beget, comprise, surprise, comprehend, apprehend, prey,* and even the word *guess*.

Be all that you can be: This campaign from the U.S. Army spotlights the verb *be*. *Be* takes many forms, to wit:

- Was

- Were

- Been

- Being

- Am

- Are

- Is, and

- Be

Words related to *be* include *yes, essence, becoming, being, existing, reality, true, sin, virtuous, improve, quintessence,* even *swastika* from the original Sanskrit *svasti* meaning "good or well-being"—which the Nazis certainly redefined.

So the Army's longtime slogan, "Be all that you can

Various Ways Shakespeare (and Others) Spelled His Name During His Lifetime and Shortly Thereafter

Shakespeare	Shaxspere
Shak-speare	Shexpere
Shake-speare	Shakspe
Shakespere	Shaxpere
Shakespear	Shagspere
Shakspeare	Shaxpeare
Shackspeare	Shaxper
Shaksper	Shakespe
Shakspere	Shakp
Shackespeare	Schaksp.
Shackspere	Shakespheare
Shaxberd	Shakespe

be," can be construed as "Have a life or reality that you can exist in actuality."

Ultimately, the word *be* stems from the Proto-Indo-European *es* (for "to be"). Perhaps the most famous use of the verb *be*, with which most English-language readers would be familiar is the "To be or not to be" soliloquy in Shakespeare's *Hamlet*.

99 AND 44/100% PURE: An advertising slogan that has outlived everyone on the planet who was able to read at the time it was introduced by the Procter & Gamble

Co. in 1882 to trumpet Ivory Soap. In the early twenty-first century, a product that is .066 impure would be considered unmarketable. In the late nineteenth century, however, this was considered the height of purity.

Swoosh: Nike's longtime "Just do it" campaign for its running shoes and sports-related apparel is always accompanied by its trademarked "swoosh." Use of onomatopoeic terms in advertising is not unknown, especially where commercials for dog and cat foods are involved. However, few have had the lasting, and global, impact of the Nike swoosh. I *swoosh*; you *swoosh*; he, she, or it *swooshes*.

The major dictionaries provide no given etymologies. Apparently, the Proto-Indo-Europeans did not *swoosh* (to move with or make a rushing sound or to swirl copiously).

Advertising Gaffes: American Chinglish?

Perhaps the most famous advertising gaffe from a major American manufacturer was that of General Motors' Chevrolet division back in the 1960s, when it shipped its Nova to Latin American markets. Of course, anyone with a rudimentary knowledge of Spanish knows that *no va* means "does not go."

So major automobile companies, with their research departments spending millions of dollars, must not make this type of rudimentary mistake anymore. Right?

Wrong. Volkswagen's naming agency probably thought the impossible-to-spell Touareg would evoke the same spirit of adventure as

(continued)

Tundra, Safari, or Denali, all names of popular off-road vehicles. In fact, Touareg, a variant spelling of Tuareg, is the name of a stateless tribe. It literally means "abandoned by God."

Coca-Cola probably thought "Coke adds life" would translate globally with only a few tweaks. So they were surprised to learn that the Chinese translation—"Coke brings the dead back to life!"—was not well received by the ancestor-worshipping Chinese.

A similar thing happened to Coca-Cola during an earlier excursion into the Chinese marketplace. In the 1920s, their advertising slogan translated into something like "bite the wax tadpole" or "female horse stuffed with wax." Either way, not good.

Finally, a Shanghai professor came up with a preferable slogan: "Happiness in the mouth."

CHAPTER SEVEN

High-Tech English

The Languages of Science and the Internet

Some time ago I taught scientific and technological communications at the University of Massachusetts. At the time this was a rather esoteric course, mainly for engineers or those in the process of becoming engineers. The topics under discussion were how to make technology readily accessible to those not initiated into the jargon of the various fields of engineering. The distinctions were civil engineering, electrical engineering, nuclear engineering, and the like. I was surprised to see that engineers in slightly differing fields often felt like total strangers when confronted with the jargon of a related field. After all, what is the precise difference between electronic and electrical engineering? It reminded me of an old bumper sticker, "Honk if you know the difference between satire and irony."

Flash forward fifteen years to witness the impact technological words have had upon the English language landscape. Now *everyone* is using the electrical engineering buzzwords, as EE has transformed into computer science, yet few always understand what these buzzwords actually mean.

**THE 10 MOST CONFUSING (YET FREQUENTLY USED)
HIGH-TECH WORDS OF 2007**

If you've heard one or more of the terms below and been awash
in confusion, or if you've *used* one or more of the terms below and
hoped no one would ask for a definition, chances are you're not
alone. These are the most commonly and incorrectly used high-
tech buzzwords around.

1. *iPod*: We all know the brand, but what exactly is a
   "pod"? A gathering of marine mammals? The encase-
   ment for peas? The evacuation module from *2001: A
   Space Odyssey?*

2. *Flash*: As in *flash memory.* This is easier to say than "I
   brought the report on my EEPROM chip with a thin
   oxide layer separating a floating gate and control gate
   utilizing Fowler-Nordheim electron tunneling."

3. *Nano*: Widely used to describe anything very small, as
   in *nanotechnology.* Like the word *mini,* which originally
   referred to the red hues in Italian *miniature* paintings,
   the word *nano* is ultimately derived from the ancient
   Greek word for *dwarf.*

4. *Cookie*: Without cookies with their "persistent state"
   management mechanism, the Web as we know it
   would cease to exist.

5. *Kernel*: The core layer of a computer operating system
   serving as a connection to the underlying hardware.
   Ultimately derives from the Old English *cyrnel* for
   corn.

6. *Megahertz (MHz)*: Named after German physicist
   Heinrich Hertz, signifying a million cycles per second

in computer processor (and not clock) speed. Next up: GigaHertz (GHz) and TeraHertz (THz), one billion and one trillion cycles.

7. *Cell* (as in cell phone): Operating on the principle of cells, which communicate through low-power transceivers to cellular towers up to seven miles away (which is why you can connect to ground stations from airplanes at 35,000 feet). The phone connects to the strongest signal, which is then passed from tower to tower.

8. *Plasma* (as in plasma television): A top word in the last survey still confusing large-screen TV buyers.

9. *De-duplication*: One of the newer buzzwords meaning removing duplicated data from a storage device, as in "We're in the process of de-duping the silo." Ouch!

10. *Blu-Ray* (vs. HD DVD). New technology for high capacity DVDs reminiscent of the VHS/Beta wars of the 1980s.

Other terms being tracked included Bluetooth, terabyte, memory, core, and head crash.

OTHER CONFUSING (YET FREQUENTLY USED) HIGH-TECH WORDS OF THE RECENT PAST

BEST OF BREED: Not to be confused with the Westminster Dog Show. A computer system (or solution) made of components from various manufacturers, a sort of high-tech mix-and-match.

DATA MIGRATION: The idea that data in your present software programs can be moved to newer and better programs without causing much of a fuss. A highly unlikely result.

HTTP: Hypertext transfer protocol is used for HTML (Hypertext markup language) files. Not to be confused with *text hyper* because of drinking too much Starbucks.

MEGAPIXEL: A really big pixel? No, one million pixels. OK, what's a pixel? Computerese for "picture element."

PLASMA: As in "Plasma TV," a flat, lightweight surface covered with millions of tiny glass bubbles. A digitally controlled electric current flowing through the surface causes the plasma inside the bubbles to glow. Not related to Red Cross blood drives.

ROBUST: No one quite knows what this means, but it's good for your technological product to demonstrate robustness.

VIRAL MARKETING: Marketing that makes your computer ill? Actually, a marketing fad that utilizes e-mail and the Internet to (theoretically) result in a geometric progression of one's marketing message. Sometimes stealthy, always irritating.

VOICE OVER IP: An acronyn for "voice over Internet protocol," VoIP (rhymes with Detroit) refers to the transmission of Internet phone calls from one Internet address to another.

WORM: A virus, right? No, a "write once, read many" file system used by computers.

Internet-related words are becoming ever more commonplace in the contemporary lexicon. Since I started working in the technological arena some two decades ago, I've participated in every technological "wave," from the late '70s until today in the late '00s (double naughts). This has provided me with a premier vantage point from which to view the intersection of technology and language. The World Wide Web came into existence for most people with the introduction of the "mosaic" interface, which allowed us to visualize information with the use of the first GUIs (pronounced "gooeys"). It was in the winter of '94–'95 that I first saw a URL (universal resource locator) posted on the side of a truck in Hopkins, Minnesota. It contained a rather rude remark. It asked: "How do you like my driving? Send comments to www.eat*?/@.com." Of course, the cleverness was not to be found in the vulgarity but rather in the fact that a URL was now considered understandable by the public.

THE 5 TOP INTERNET-RELATED WORDS

1. *LOL:* Lots of love? Laughing out loud? Lots of luck? This chat- and gameroom acronym can substitute for any of the above, so you have to figure it out from context.

2. *Code kiddies:* This new appellation for hackers betrays their fall in esteem.

3. *Steganography:* Hiding things in plain view. Watermarks on graphics and other hidden identifiers on Web pages have brought forth a new science for the protection of intellectual property.

Some Internet Words Moving into Widespread Use

IM: Instant Message.

Multitask: To perform several tasks at the same time; now a requirement of all non-outsourced jobs.

Offline: What happens after you've been multitasking too long.

4. *Emoticon:* A blend of "emotion" and "icon." (For some interesting examples of emoticons, see chapter 5, page 98.)

5. *Thingy:* As opposed to "thing," this term refers to all those new objects associated with computers and computer screens for which normal men and women have no words. It isn't new, but its usage has soared as people take the Internet plunge.

THE TOP LANGUAGES OF THE INTERNET

English is the most frequently used language on the Internet, with about 300 million users. What follows are the rest of the most popular languages in cyberspace, with approximate number of users (and percentage of total users).

English:	300 million (30%)
Chinese:	150 million (15%)
Japanese:	90 million (9%)
Spanish:	60 million (6%)

German:	60 million (6%)
French:	40 million (4%)
Korean:	30 million (3%)
Portuguese:	30 million (3%)
Italian:	30 million (3%)
Russian:	20 million (2%)

**Native Language of Those Who Have
Access to the Internet (2006)**

➤ *37.9% European languages (excluding English)*
➤ *35.8% English*
➤ *33.0% Asian languages*

Years ago, men would stand around their "muscle cars" and impress each other with the size, horsepower, number of cylinders, valves, displacement in cubic inches, and such. Today with the greening of the planet, such boasting is made for "rice rockets," the smaller yet powerful vehicles of East Asian design. And the tradition continues with "cyber-cycles," those "tricked-out" or "souped-up" personal computers.

COMPUTER POWER!

How much power does your computer have? Just imagine what it could do if it had a yottabyte! That's right: a yottabyte is a lotta bytes.

Mega—Million

Giga—Billion

Tera—Trillion

Peta—Quadrillion

Exa—Quintillion

Zetta—Septillion

Yotta—Sextillion

Beyond yotta: Wicked fast!

AMOUNT OF DIGITIZED INFORMATION

Now, how much information can your computer store? And do you really need to carry around enough storage to duplicate the Library of Congress on your laptop?

Kilobyte (KB): 1,000 bytes
   2 kilobytes: A typewritten page
   100 kilobytes: A low-resolution photograph

Megabyte (MB): 1,000,000 bytes
   3 megabytes: King James Bible
   5 megabytes: Shakespeare's complete works

Gigabyte (GB): 1,000,000,000 bytes
   100 gigabytes: Library floor of academic journals

Terabyte (TB): 1,000,000,000,000 bytes
   10 terabytes: U.S. Library of Congress (print)

Petabyte (PB): 1,000,000,000,000,000 bytes
   200 petabytes: All the printed material in the world

Galaxies

There are one hundred billion stars in the Milky Way Galaxy (*galaxy* is from the Greek for "milky," so the actual name of our galaxy is closer to the "Milky Milky"). There are also about one hundred billion galaxies. So the number of stars is about 100 billion multiplied by 100 billion. There's a name for numbers that size, as there are names for numbers of every conceivable size. The largest *named* number is often thought to be the googol: One followed by 100 zeros. But it turns out that the googol is actually the *penultimate* named number. The largest named number is actually the *googolplex*, which is a googol of googols. This terminology was created by the nephew of American mathematician Edward Kasner (as discussed in chapter 6, page 121).

Exabyte (EB): 1,000,000,000,000,000,000 bytes

5 Exabytes: All words ever spoken by all human beings

A British Billion
When you cross the "Pond," the powers of ten takes on an added dimension. A British billion is a million millions rather than the thousand millions its is in America, while a British trillion is a million billions rather than our million millions.

Powers of Ten (American System)

NAME	POWER OF 10	NUMBER OF ZEROS
Ten	10^1	1
Hundred	10^2	2
Thousand	10^3	3
Million	10^6	6
Billion	10^9	9
Trillion	10^{12}	12
Quadrillion	10^{15}	15
Quintillion	10^{18}	18
Sextillion	10^{21}	21
Septillion	10^{24}	24
Octillion	10^{27}	27
Nonillion	10^{30}	30
Decellion	10^{33}	33
Undecillion	10^{36}	36
Duodecillion	10^{39}	39
Tredecillion	10^{42}	42
Quattuordecillion	10^{45}	45
Quindecillion	10^{48}	48
Sexdecillion	10^{51}	51
Septdecillion	10^{54}	54
Octodecillion	10^{57}	57
Novemdecillion	10^{60}	60
Vigintillion	10^{63}	63
Googol	10^{100}	100
Quintoquadagintillion	10^{138}	138
Centillion	10^{303}	303
Googolplex	10^{googol}	10^{100}

Googol vs. Google

The mathematical term googol *was coined by the nine-year-old nephew of American mathematician Edward Kasner. The technical name for this number is* duotrigintillion.
As for the name of the search engine, Google was, ironically, an inadvertent misspelling of googol *during a domain name search. Google was available, so founders Larry Page and Sergey Brin registered it for their business on September 15, 1997*

ORIGINS OF THE ENGLISH NAMES FOR NUMBERS

ONE: Greek *eis*, Latin *unus*. Derivatives include: unit, once, atone, union, universe, any.

Two: Greek *dyo*, Latin *duo*, Middle English *twa*. Derivatives include: twin, twilight, twain, biscuit, between, combine, dichotomy, diploma, duet, double, doubt (of two minds).

THREE: Greek *treis*, Anglo-Saxon *thrī*. Derivatives include: trefoil, trio, trinity, trident, tripod, triangle, triple, thirteen, thirty.

FOUR: Greek *tettares*, Latin *quattuor*, Anglo-Saxon *fēower*. Derivatives include: squad, fortnight, quatrain, quadruple, quadruped, quart, quarter, quartet, quarto, fourteen, forty.

FIVE: Greek *pente*, Latin *quinque*, Anglo-Saxon *fīf*. Derivatives include: fifth (liquor), finger, foist,

Pentecost, Pentagon, Pentateuch, quintuple, quintessence, quincunx, fifteen, fifty.

Six: Greek *hex*, Latin *sex*. Derivatives include: hexagon, sextuplet, sextet, semester, sixteen, sixty.

Seven: Greek *hepta*, Latin *septem*, Anglo-Saxon *seofon*. Derivatives include: septet, September, heptagon, hephtathion, seventeen, seventy, septuagenarian.

Quintessence: *That substance found beyond the Earth of which the heavenly bodies are composed. Earth consisted of the Four Elements: Earth, Air, Fire, and Water. The heavenly bodies were composed of the Fifth Essence or Element. Hence the term quintessential.*

Eight: Greek *octo*, Latin *octo*, Anglo-Saxon *eahta*. Derivatives include: octave, octopus, octago, October, eighteen, eighty, octogenarian.

Nine: Greek *ennea*, Latin *novem*, Old Norse German *neun*. Derivatives include: novena, nanosecond, November, nineteen, ninety, nonogenarian.

Ten: Greek *deka*, Latin decem, Anglo-Saxon *tīen*. Derivatives include dean, decimal, decimate, December.

Hundred: Greek *hekaton*, Latin *centum*, Anglo-Saxon *hundred*. Derivatives include: cent, century, centipede, Centigrade, hecacomb, hectogram.

Thousand: Greek *chilioi*, Latin *mille*, Anglo-Saxon *thūsend*. Derivatives include mile, millennium, milligram.

MYRIAD: The ancient Greek name for ten thousand; their largest named number was a myriad myriad, or a million.

To **decimate** does not mean to kill everyone! It was a Roman punishment for rebelling cities: to line up all the men and kill every tenth person in line; i.e., only 10 percent of the total assembled.

String Theory

Sometimes the world of science presents us with a new idea or set of ideas that's so strange, so alien to our current way of thinking, that a whole new set of vocabulary needs to be developed to talk about it. String theory is an example of this. String theory is the theory that the universe is made of tiny, vibrating "strings" of energy. It maintains that in spite of the fact that we live in a world of four dimensions, there are actually eleven dimensions. String theory also engenders the possibility that there are parallel universes, operating in the same space in which we live; it's just that we can't see the other dimensions. Right now, the language of string theory and other esoteric branches of science is primarily used only by scientists. But who knows, maybe a decade from now, these words will have become a common part of the language.

TOP 10 WORDS RELATING TO STRING THEORY

1. *Particles:* The fundamental, or elementary, building blocks of all matter.

2. *Relativity:* The necessity of a context or a system to determine what is meaningful or significant.

3. *Graviton:* A hypothetical elementary particle that transmits the force of gravity in most quantum gravity systems.

4. *M-theory:* The theory of an eleven-dimensional universe, in which the weak and strong forces and gravity are unified. All the string theories fall into the category of M-theory.

5. *Hadrons:* Subatomic particles that are composed of quarks. There are hundreds of hadrons, two of which are the all-too-familiar proton and neutron.

6. *Torus:* When two circles spin about themselves they form a mathematical object called a torus. A torus looks like a real-world donut.

7. *Tachyons:* From the Greek word meaning "swift," the tachyon is a particle that theoretically travels faster than light.

8. *Planck length:* The size of a typical string in string theory.

9. *Supersymmetry:* A theory stating that every particle has a supersymmetric partner. Of course, none of these "shadow particles" have been detected.

10. *Bosonic string theory:* The original version of string theory from the late 1960s. It postulates that a particle (a tachyon) travels faster than light. None of these particles have ever been observed.

As the scientific and technological worlds become more closely interlinked with everyday life, we will notice an ever greater num-

The Mathematical Basis of Yogi-isms

Lawrence Peter "Yogi" Berra, a Hall of Fame catcher during the heyday of the great New York Yankee baseball dynasty of the '50s, was known for his interesting way of constructing sentences. These became widely known as "Yogi-isms."

What has not been previously understood is the mathematical basis of his thought. Three examples follow:

1. Yogi said: "Ninety percent of baseball is half mental."
Given: mental = .9; physical = .5
.9 x .5 = .45
Therefore, it can be demonstrated that, according to Yogi, baseball is
    actually 45 percent mental and 55 percent physical.

2. Yogi said: "It ain't over 'til it's over."
Probability that "it" is over before "it" has completed its cycle or func-
    tion (that is, "is over") = 0 percent probability.
Probability that "it" is over once "it" has actually completed its cycle or
    function (that is, "is over") = 100 percent
Thus we have demonstrated the mathematical validity of the state-
    ment: "It ain't over 'til it's over."

3. Yogi said: "If you come to a fork in the road, take it."
Given: A fork in the road is defined as a road bifurcating into two
    roads, each with a differing direction.
When a man is traveling along said road and approaches said fork, for
    him to proceed forward, he must take only one of the forks.
In this thoroughly randomized sample, there is a 50 percent probability
    that he will take one of the forks. Thus, the probability that he will
    take either of the forks while moving forward approaches 100 per-
    cent.

Q.E.D.

ber of technological terms positioning themselves comfortably within everyday speech. If you find yourself in a conversation about bosonic string theory or the mathematical basis of Yogi-isms, rest content with the fact that you're venturing into a territory never imagined by Shakespeare, Jane Austen, Charles Dickens, Joseph Conrad, or F. Scott Fitzgerald, as Global English continues to expand beyond the pale of our collective imaginations.

CHAPTER EIGHT

Language by the Numbers

Language Stats

Reliable language statistics are notoriously difficult to come by. Since they can be the basis of government funding, educational grants, research fellowships, and the like, institutions are incentivized to present certain statistical profiles that open up additional funding opportunities. Nevertheless, this chapter contains a number of language statistics that you will find interesting, for they demonstrate, to some degree, how Global English is positioned in the world.

NUMBER OF WORDS IN OTHER LANGUAGES AND OTHER LANGUAGE STATISTICS

AVERAGE AMERICAN VOCABULARY: 16,000 words (consensus estimate)

AVERAGE WORDS RECOGNIZED BY HIGHLY EDUCATED ENGLISH SPEAKERS: 75,000 words+

AVERAGE NEWSPAPER VOCABULARY: 6,000 words

SHAKESPEARE'S VOCABULARY: 24,000 words+ (various concordances)

NUMBER OF WORDS (NEOLOGISMS) INVENTED BY SHAKESPEARE: 1,700+

NUMBER OF WORDS INVENTED BY THOMAS JEFFERSON: 150

NUMBER OF WORDS INVENTED BY PRESIDENT BUSH: 25+

The estimated number of living languages is 6,912. This number, compiled by the Ethnologue organization, is considered by the academic world to be the most accurate. This is not to say that there aren't obscure languages on the verge of extinction, spoken by only handfuls of people, which have yet to be discovered. However, as communications media becomes ever more available, this possibility becomes less and less likely.

The estimated number of languages, dialects, pidgin, patois, etc. is 39,491

ESTIMATED NUMBER OF WORDS IN VARIOUS WORLD LANGUAGES

As we noted earlier, there is evidence that languages are genuinely alive insofar as they are born, grow, shed words, morph, evolve, and die in a very lifelike manner. They also have their own personalities. Some are very verbose; some seem rather reticent, using the minimum of words to convey the thoughts they encapsulate; still others splinter into any number of dialects, which can hinder the long-term survival of the language. This is what happened to Latin, splintering into the Romance languages (Italian, Spanish, Portuguese, French, et cetera). However, Greek has remained basically the same language since antiquity. There are no current native speakers of Latin; there are millions of native speakers of Greek.

Belarus: Minsk

Belgium: Brussels

Belize: Belmopan

Benin: Porto-Novo

Bhutan: Thimphu

Bolivia: La Paz (administrative); Sucre (judicial)

Bosnia and Herzegovina: Sarajevo

Botswana: Gaborone

Brazil: Brasilia

Brunei: Bandar Seri Begawan

Bulgaria: Sofia

Burkina Faso: Ouagadougou

Burundi: Bujumbura

Cambodia: Phnom Penh

Cameroon: Yaounde

Canada: Ottawa

Cape Verde: Praia

Central African Republic: Bangui

Chad: N'Djamena

Chile: Santiago

China: Beijing

Colombia: Bogotà

Comoros: Moroni

Congo, Republic of the: Brazzaville

Congo, Democratic Republic of the: Kinshasa

Costa Rica: San Jose

Cote d'Ivoire: Yamoussoukro (official); Abidjan (de facto)

Croatia: Zagreb

Cuba: Havana

Cyprus: Nicosia

Czech Republic: Prague

Denmark: Copenhagen

Djibouti: Djibouti

Dominica: Roseau

Dominican Republic: Santo Domingo

East Timor: Dili

Ecuador: Quito

Egypt: Cairo

El Salvador: San Salvador

Chinese (various dialects): 500,000+

French: 100,000

German: 185,000

Russian: 195,000

Spanish: 275,000+

Japanese: 232,000

Hindi: 120,000

Arabic: 45,000

There are 194 countries in the world. Most people c[...]
more than fifty of these nations. I'm listing them now, [...]
can see the diversity of cultures when we speak about ho[...]
guages are spoken in which countries.

THE COUNTRIES OF THE WORLD
AND THEIR CAPITAL CITIES

Afghanistan: Kabul

Albania: Tirane

Algeria: Algiers

Andorra: Andorra la Vella

Angola: Luanda

Antigua and Barbuda:
Saint John's

Argentina: Buenos Aires

Armenia: Yerevan

Australia: Canberr[...]

Austria: Vienna

Azerbaijan: Baku

The Bahamas: Na[...]

Bahrain: Manama

Bangladesh: Dhak[...]

Barbados: Bridge[...]

Equatorial Guinea: Malabo

Eritrea: Asmara

Estonia: Tallinn

Ethiopia: Addis Ababa

Fiji: Suva

Finland: Helsinki

France: Paris

Gabon: Libreville

The Gambia: Banjul

Georgia: Tbilisi

Germany: Berlin

Ghana: Accra

Greece: Athens

Grenada: Saint George's

Guatemala: Guatemala City

Guinea: Conakry

Guinea-Bissau: Bissau

Guyana: Georgetown

Haiti: Port-au-Prince

Honduras: Tegucigalpa

Hungary: Budapest

Iceland: Reykjavik

India: New Delhi

Indonesia: Jakarta

Iran: Tehran

Iraq: Baghdad

Ireland: Dublin

Israel: Jerusalem

Italy: Rome

Jamaica: Kingston

Japan: Tokyo

Jordan: Amman

Kazakhstan: Astana

Kenya: Nairobi

Kiribati: Tarawa Atoll

Korea, North: Pyongyang

Korea, South: Seoul

Kuwait: Kuwait City

Kyrgyzstan: Bishkek

Laos: Vientiane

Latvia: Riga

Lebanon: Beirut

Lesotho: Maseru

Liberia: Monrovia

Libya: Tripoli

Liechtenstein: Vaduz

Lithuania: Vilnius

Luxembourg: Luxembourg

Macedonia: Skopje

Madagascar: Antananarivo

Malawi: Lilongwe

Malaysia: Kuala Lumpur

Maldives: Male

Mali: Bamako

Malta: Valletta

Marshall Islands: Majuro

Mauritania: Nouakchott

Mauritius: Port Louis

Mexico: Mexico City

Federated States of
Micronesia: Palikir

Moldova: Chisinau

Monaco: Monaco

Mongolia: Ulaanbaatar

Montenegro: Podgorica

Morocco: Rabat

Mozambique: Maputo

Myanmar (Burma): Rangoon
(Yangon); Nay Pyi Taw
(administrative)

Namibia: Windhoek

Nauru: no official capital;
government offices in Yaren
District

Nepal: Kathmandu

Netherlands: Amsterdam; The
Hague (seat of government)

New Zealand: Wellington

Nicaragua: Managua

Niger: Niamey

Nigeria: Abuja

Norway: Oslo

Oman: Muscat

Pakistan: Islamabad

Palau: Melekeok

Panama: Panama City

Papua New Guinea:
Port Moresby

Paraguay: Asuncion

Peru: Lima

Philippines: Manila

Poland: Warsaw

Portugal: Lisbon

Qatar: Doha

Romania: Bucharest

Russia: Moscow

Rwanda: Kigali

Saint Kitts and Nevis: Basseterre

Saint Lucia: Castries

Saint Vincent and the Grenadines: Kingstown

Samoa: Apia

San Marino: San Marino

São Tomé and Principe: São Tomé

Saudi Arabia: Riyadh

Senegal: Dakar

Serbia: Belgrade

Seychelles: Victoria

Sierra Leone: Freetown

Singapore: Singapore

Slovakia: Bratislava

Slovenia: Ljubljana

Solomon Islands: Honiara

Somalia: Mogadishu

South Africa: Pretoria (administrative); Cape Town (legislative); Bloemfontein (judiciary)

Spain: Madrid

Sri Lanka: Colombo; Sri Jayewardenepura Kotte (legislative)

Sudan: Khartoum

Suriname: Paramaribo

Swaziland: Mbabana

Sweden: Stockholm

Switzerland: Bern

Syria: Damascus

Taiwan: Taipei

Tajikistan: Dushanbe

Tanzania: Dar es Salaam; Dodoma (legislative)

Thailand: Bangkok

Togo: Lome

Tonga: Nuku'alofa

Trinidad and Tobago:
Port-of-Spain

Tunisia: Tunis

Turkey: Ankara

Turkmenistan: Ashgabat

Tuvalu: Vaiaku village,
Funafuti province

Uganda: Kampala

Ukraine: Kyiv

United Arab Emirates:
Abu Dhabi

United Kingdom: London

United States: Washington,
D.C.

Uruguay: Montevideo

Uzbekistan: Tashkent

Vanuatu: Port-Vila

Vatican City (Holy See):
Vatican City

Venezuela: Caracas

Vietnam: Hanoi

Yemen: Sanaa

Zambia: Lusaka

Zimbabwe: Harare

OFFICIAL LANGUAGES RANKED BY NUMBER OF COUNTRIES (WITH SURPRISES NOTED)

Note: Many countries have more than one official language.

ENGLISH: 52 countries
- largest: India, United States, Pakistan (where's England?)

FRENCH: 29 countries
- largest: France, Democratic Republic of the Congo, Canada (the Congo is no. 2?)

ARABIC: 24 countries
- largest: Egypt, Sudan, Algeria (where's Iran? Its natives speak Persian or Farsi—not Arabic!)

SPANISH: 20 countries
- largest: Mexico, Spain, Colombia (where's Brazil? see below.)

PORTUGUESE: 8 countries
- largest: Brazil, Mozambique, Angola (where's Portugal?)

GERMAN: 6 countries

ITALIAN, RUSSIAN: 4 countries

CHINESE, DUTCH, MALAY, PERSIAN, SERBIAN, SWAHILI, TAMIL, URDU: 3 countries

ALBANIAN, AYMARA, BENGALI, CROATIAN, GREEK, HINDI, JAPANESE, KOREAN, QUECHUA, ROMANIAN, SOTHO, SWAZI, SWEDISH, TSWANA, TURKISH: each 2 countries

Numerous languages: 1 country

Languages by World Region

IN AFRICA

FRENCH, SPOKEN IN 22 COUNTRIES: Algeria, Benin, Burkina Faso, Burundi, Cameroon, Central African Republic, Chad, Côte d'Ivoire, Democratic Republic of the Congo, Djibouti, Equatorial Guinea, Gabon, Guinea, Madagascar, Mali, Mauritania, Mauritius, Morocco, Niger, Rwanda, Senegal, and Tunisia

ENGLISH, SPOKEN IN 22 COUNTRIES: Botswana, Cameroon, Eritrea, Ethiopia, Gambia, Ghana, Kenya, Lesotho, Liberia, Malawi, Mauritius, Namibia, Nigeria, Rwanda, Sierra Leone, Somalia, South Africa, Swaziland, Tanzania, Uganda, Zambia, and Zimbabwe

ARABIC, SPOKEN IN 12 COUNTRIES: Algeria, Chad, Djibouti, Egypt, Eritrea, Libya, Morocco, Oman, Somalia, Sudan, Tanzania, and Tunisia

SWAHILI, SPOKEN IN 9 COUNTRIES: Burundi, Kenya, Mozambique, Oman, Rwanda, Somalia, South Africa, Tanzania, and Uganda

PORTUGUESE, SPOKEN IN 6 COUNTRIES: Angola, Cape Verde Islands, Congo, Guinea-Bissau, Malawi, and Mozambique

SWAZI OR SWATI, SPOKEN IN 4 COUNTRIES: Swaziland, Lesotho, Mozambique, and South Africa

TSWANA, SPOKEN IN 4 COUNTRIES: Botswana, Namibia, South Africa, and Zimbabwe

SOTHO, SPOKEN IN 3 COUNTRIES: Lesotho, Botswana, and South Africa

IN THE AMERICAS

ENGLISH, SPOKEN IN 30 COUNTRIES: Antigua, Aruba, Bahamas, Barbados, Belize, Bermuda, British Virgin Islands, Canada, Cayman Islands, Dominica, Dominican Republic, Ecuador, Falkland Islands, Grenada, Guadeloupe, Guyana, Honduras, Jamaica, Mexico, Montserrat, Netherlands Antilles, Saint Kitts and Nevis, Saint Lucia, Saint Pierre and Miquelon, Saint Vincent and the Grenadines, Trinidad and Tobago, Turks and Caicos Islands, USA, Vanuatu, and Venezuela

SPANISH, SPOKEN IN 19 COUNTRIES: Argentina, Aruba, Belize, Bolivia, Canada, Cayman Islands, Chile, Colombia, Costa Rica, Cuba, Dominican Republic, Ecuador, E1 Salvador, Guatemala, Honduras, Mexico, Nicaragua, Venezuela, and USA

PORTUGUESE, SPOKEN IN 6 COUNTRIES: Antigua, Brazil, Canada, Guyana, Jamaica, and São Tomé e Principe

FRENCH, SPOKEN IN 5 COUNTRIES: Canada, Haiti, Martinique, Saint Pierre and Miquelon, USA

AYMARA, SPOKEN IN 4 COUNTRIES: Argentina, Bolivia, Chile, and Peru

DUTCH, SPOKEN IN 2 COUNTRIES: Netherland Antilles and Suriname

QUECHUA, SPOKEN IN 1 COUNTRY: Peru

LANGUAGES SPOKEN IN ASIA

ENGLISH, SPOKEN IN 16 COUNTRIES: Brunei, Cambodia, China, India, Israel, Japan, South Korea, Lebanon, Malaysia (Peninsular), Pakistan, Philippines, Saudi Arabia, Singapore, Solomon Islands, Sri Lanka, and the United Arab Emirates

KOREAN, SPOKEN IN 16 COUNTRIES: Bahrain, Brunei, China, Japan, Kazakhstan, North Korea, Kyrgyzstan,

New Zealand, Philippines, Russia (Asia), Saudi Arabia, Singapore, Tajikistan, Thailand, Turkmenistan, and Uzbekistan

PERSIAN, SPOKEN IN 14 COUNTRIES: Azerbaijan, Bahrain, India, Iraq, Iran, Israel, Oman, Qatar, Saudi Arabia, Tajikistan, Turkey (Asia), Turkmenistan, United Arab Emirates, and Uzbekistan

CHINESE, SPOKEN IN 12 COUNTRIES: Brunei, Cambodia, Indonesia (Java and Bali), Laos, Malaysia (Peninsular), Mongolia, Philippines, Russia (Asia), Singapore, Taiwan, Thailand, and Vietnam

ARABIC, SPOKEN IN 13 COUNTRIES: Bahrain, Eritrea, Iraq, Israel, Jordan, Kuwait, Lebanon, Libya, Oman, Qatar, Syria, United Arab Emirates, and Yemen

URDU, SPOKEN IN 11 COUNTRIES: Afghanistan, Bahrain, Bangladesh, India, Nepal, Oman, Pakistan, Qatar, Saudi Arabia, Thailand, and UAE

RUSSIAN, SPOKEN IN 10 COUNTRIES: Armenia, Azerbaijan, Belarus, China, Georgia, India, Israel, Kazakhstan, Kyrgyzstan, and Moldova

MALAY, SPOKEN IN 7 COUNTRIES: Brunei, Indonesia, Malaysia, Myanmar, Singapore, Thailand, and UAE

TAMIL, SPOKEN IN 8 COUNTRIES: Bahrain, India, Malaysia (Peninsular), Qatar, Singapore, Sri Lanka, Thailand, and UAE

BENGALI, SPOKEN IN 6 COUNTRIES: Bangladesh, India, Nepal, Saudi Arabia, Singapore, and United Arab Emirates

IN EUROPE

GERMAN, SPOKEN IN 17 COUNTRIES: Austria, Belgium, Bosnia, Czech Republic, Denmark, Estonia, Finland, France, Germany, Hungary, Italy, Liechtenstein, Luxembourg, Poland, Romania, Russia (Europe), Slovakia, and Ukraine

GREEK, SPOKEN IN 16 COUNTRIES: Albania, Armenia, Austria, Bulgaria, Cyprus, France, Georgia, Germany, Greece, Hungary, Italy, Poland, Romania, Russia (Europe), Sweden, and Ukraine

POLISH, SPOKEN IN 15 COUNTRIES: Austria, Azerbaijan, Belarus, Czech Republic, Estonia, Finland, Germany, Hungary, Latvia, Lithuania, Poland, Romania, Russia (Europe), Slovakia, and Ukraine

ITALIAN, SPOKEN IN 14 COUNTRIES: Belgium, Bosnia, Croatia, France, Germany, Italy, Liechtenstein, Luxembourg, Romania, San Marino, Slovenia, Switzerland, United Kingdom, and the Vatican State

RUSSIAN, SPOKEN IN 14 COUNTRIES: Armenia, Azerbaijan, Belarus, Bulgaria, Czech Republic, Estonia, Finland, Georgia, Germany, Greece, Latvia, Lithuania, Moldova, and Russia

SERBIAN, SPOKEN IN 13 COUNTRIES: Albania, Bosnia, Bulgaria, Greece, Macedonia, Montenegro, Romania, Russia (Europe), Serbia, Sweden, Switzerland, Turkey (Europe), and Ukraine

FRENCH, SPOKEN IN 10 COUNTRIES: Andorra, Austria, Belgium, France, Hungary, Italy, Luxembourg, Monaco, Switzerland, and the United Kingdom

ENGLISH, SPOKEN IN 8 COUNTRIES: Germany, Gibraltar, Greece, Ireland, Italy, Malta, Switzerland, and United Kingdom

HUNGARIAN, SPOKEN IN 8 COUNTRIES: Austria, Hungary, Montenegro, Romania, Serbia, Slovakia, Slovenia, and Ukraine. (Note: Hungarian is a member of the Uralic language family, and is related to Finnish.)

ROMANIAN, SPOKEN IN 8 COUNTRIES: Azerbaijan, Finland, Hungary, Montenegro, Romania, Russia (Europe), Serbia, and Ukraine

CROATIAN, SPOKEN IN 7 COUNTRIES: Austria, Bosnia, Germany, Hungary, Italy, Slovakia, and Slovenia

ALBANIAN, SPOKEN IN 6 COUNTRIES: Albania, Belgium, Germany, Sweden, Turkey (Europe), and Ukraine. (Note: Many Albanian linguists believe their language is descended from the Egyptian.)

FINNISH, SPOKEN IN 5 COUNTRIES: Estonia, Finland, Norway, Russia (Europe), and Sweden. (Note: Finnish is not related to any other language except Hungarian.)

SWEDISH, SPOKEN IN 4 COUNTRIES: Estonia, Finland, Norway, and Sweden

DUTCH, SPOKEN IN 4 COUNTRIES: Belgium, France, Germany, and the Netherlands

BASQUE, SPOKEN IN 1 COUNTRY: Spain. (Note: Like Finnish, Basque is another language isolate.)

Languages of Australia: And You Thought It Was All G'day, and Barbie, and Such!

Australia has 231 living languages.

> LIVING LANGUAGES INCLUDE: Afrikaans, Assyrian Neo-Aramaic, Basque, Chaldean Eastern Yiddish, Fijian Hindustani, Greek, Hebrew, Indo-Portuguese, Italian, Lao, Latvian, Maltese, Mambae, Northern Kurdish (11,000), Northern Uzbek, Nung, Polish, Pukapuka, Scottish Gaelic, Senaya, Sylheti, Tai Dam, Tongan, Traveller Scottish, Turkish, Turoyo, Unserdeutsch, Uyghur, Vietnamese, and Yue Chinese, among many others.

Number of Speakers for the Top Languages

Curently, 6,912 languages are spoken in the world, and some 200 have 1 million or more speakers. There are 6.5 billion people on the globe today. Global English has about 1.35 billion total speakers, but far fewer native speakers. It is the only language spoken on all five continents.

LANGUAGES WITH THE MOST NATIVE SPEAKERS (2007 ESTIMATES)

1. Mandarin	1,050,000,000
2. English	535,000,000
3. Hindi	487,000,000
4. Arabic	475,000,000
5. Spanish	417,000,000

6. Bengali   205,000,000

7. Portuguese   200,000,000

8. Russian   158,000,000

9. Japanese   125,000,000

10. German   100,000,000

Others of note: Javanese, 86 million; Korean, 78 million; Vietnamese, 74 million; French, 65 million; Italian, 62 million.

In the United States approximately 165 languages are spoken today.

On the Island of New Guinea, some 900 languages are spoken by members of a population of fewer than 10 million.

Fewer than half the world languages are learned by the children of native speakers.

Some 2,000 languages have fewer than 1,000 speakers; hundreds have fewer than 10 speakers; scores have a single elderly speaker.

Official Languages Around the World

COUNTRIES WHOSE SOLE OFFICIAL LANGUAGE IS ENGLISH

Antigua and Barbuda   Dominica

Bahamas   Fiji

Barbados   Gambia

Belize   Ghana

Botswana   Grenada

Guyana

Jamaica

Kiribati

Lesotho

Liberia

Marshall Islands

Mauritius

Fed. States of Micronesia

Namibia

New Zealand

Nigeria

Papua New Guinea

Sts. Kitts and Nevis

St. Lucia

St. Vincent and the Grenadines

Sierra Leone

Solomon Islands

Trinidad and Tobago

Uganda

Zambia

Zimbabwe

OTHER COUNTRIES IN WHICH ENGLISH IS AN OFFICIAL LANGUAGE

Cameroon

Canada

Equatorial Guinea

India

Ireland

Kenya

Malawi

Malta

Palau

Philippines

Rwanda

Seychelles

Singapore

Sri Lanka

Swaziland

Tonga

Tuvalu

United Republic of Tanzania

United Kingdom

Vanuatu

COUNTRIES WITH NO OFFICIAL LANGUAGE

Afghanistan	Hungary
Australia	Iceland
Belarus	Korea, North
Belgium	Korea, South
Bulgaria	Mexico
Chile	Myanmar
Colombia	Nepal
Cuba	Samoa
Czech Republic	Slovenia
Denmark	South Africa
Dominican Republic	Thailand
E1 Salvador	Tuvalu
Ethiopia	United States
Germany	Uruguay
Guatemala	

APPROXIMATE NUMBER OF ENGLISH SPEAKERS IN THE WORLD

500,000,000 native speakers

850,000,000 second, third, or professional speakers

COUNTRIES WITH SIGNIFICANT NUMBERS OF
ENGLISH SPEAKERS

American Samoa
Andorra
Anguilla
Antigua and Barbuda
Aruba
Australia
Bahamas
Barbados
Belize
Bermuda
Botswana
British Virgin Islands
Brunei
Cambodia
Cameroon
Canada
Cayman Islands
China
Cok Islands
Denmark
Dominica
Dominican Republic
Ecuador
Eritrea
Ethiopia

Falkland Islands
Fiji
Finland
Gambia
Germany
Ghana
Gibraltar
Greece
Grenada
Guadeloupe
Guam
Guyana
Honduras
India
Ireland
Israel
Italy
Jamaica
Japan
Kenya
Kiribati
Lebanon
Lesotho
Liberia
Malawi
Malaysia
Malta
Marshall Islands

Mauritius
Mexico
Micronesia
Montserrat
Namibia
Nauru
Netherlands Antilles
New Zealand
Nigeria
Niue
Norfolk Island
Northern Mariana Islands
Norway
Pakistan
Palau
Papua New Guinea
Philippines
Pitcairn
Puerto Rico
Rwanda
Saint Helena
Saint Kitts and Nevis
Saint Lucia
Saint Pierre and Miquelon

Samoa
Saudi Arabia
Seychelles
Sierra Leone
Singapore
Solomon Islands
Somalia
South Africa
South Korea
Sri Lanka
Surinam
Swaziland
Switzerland
Tanzania
Tonga
Trinidad and Tobago
Turks and Caicos
U.S. Virgin Islands
Uganda
United Arab Emirates
United States
Vanuatu
Venezuela
Zambia
Zimbabwe

CHAPTER NINE

The Name Game
People, Places and Things

Just a Name

When I hear a particularly interesting name, I'll often ask the person, "What does your name mean?" to which the most typical response is, "It's just a name."

If you've learned anything thus far from this book, it is that words are never "just" words and, accordingly, names are never "just" names.

An elementary understanding of this came to me at a young age when I heard my father's single word comments on various names:

NAME	COMMENT
Madjefka	"Carrot."
Poduska	"Pillow."
Peevo	"Beer."

These were Polish surnames. My father learned Polish at home from his parents who had emigrated to New Jersey from the mountains southeast of Cracow. As you can imagine this was quite exciting to me. I soon learned that Polish surnames were invariably earthy, plainspoken, and practical. Payack, my own surname, is a variation of "pajak," which means spider, such as one who resides under the house (or sign) of the spider. Think of the whole new world I had to explore: surnames! My mother's maiden name, Marcello, is a corruption of "stone-cutter," my wife's maiden name is Lorenzo, meaning "crowned with laurels" or "champion." Her given name, Millie ultimately derives from the Middle English, "mild tryth," meaning "mild strength" in the manner that a well-made sword is "true." My own name, Paul J.J. (Joseph John) Payack means "Small Multiplying Spider Blessed by God." My pseudonym, the WordMan, means . . . , well you get the idea.

The best name etymology I've ever encountered was that of a fellow student whose actual name I can no longer remember. As we were waiting to register for a summer class, we introduced ourselves to each other. I happened to remark that her name must have a particularly interesting meaning. This being Harvard, of course she had long-ago tracked and traced it. "You are not going to believe this," she said, "but it means 'the mold that grows on cottage cheese.'" I guess that particular family was well aware that at some point in history the wonder drug penicillin would be derived from it or one of its close relatives.

This chapter is about the "back stories" of many names that we encounter every day. First, we will look at *eponyms*: words formed from names.

EPONYMOUS WORDS

ALGORITHM: A finite list of mathematical instructions, derived via its Latin transcription of the name of a ninth-century Arab mathematician, al-Khuwarizmi, who wrote a treatise about such a process.

AMERICA: Two continents, a nation, and a dream, set down in print in 1507 by mapmaker Martin Waldseemüller, who thought incorrectly that the explorer Amerigo Vespucci (1454–1512) was the first European to first set foot upon the New World.

BOUGAINVILLEA: A flowering plant, named for Louis Antoine de Bougainville, a French admiral who discovered the plant in Brazil in 1768.

CAESARIAN (C-)SECTION: A surgical procedure named for Roman emperor Julius Caesar, said to have been "plucked from his mother's womb."

CARDIGAN: A knitted, collarless jacket, named for James Thomas Brudenell (1797–1868), the 7th Earl of Cardigan, who wore such a garment. He famously led the Charge of the Light Brigade in the Crimea in 1854.

DECIBEL: A logarithmic unit of measurement of a sound's intensity, named by the Bell Telephone Laboratory during the 1920s in honor of Alexander Graham Bell, the inventor of the telephone. Normal conversation registers about 30 decibels.

EUSTACHIAN TUBE: A canal or channel that links the pharynx to the middle ear, named for Italian anatomist Bartolommeo Eustachio (1524–1574).

FALLOPIAN TUBE: An oviduct or tube leading from each ovary into the uterus, named for Eustachio's fellow anatomist Gabriel Fallopius (1523–1562).

FRISBEE: A disk-shaped toy, invented in 1955 by Fred Morrison and originally marketed as the Pluto Platter. It is believed that the toy was renamed in 1958 to honor Bridgeport, Connecticut, pie company founder William Russell Frisbie (d. 1903), whose pie pans (some say, cookie-tin lids) shared the toy's ability to spin when thrown.

JACUZZI: A trademark name for the whirlpool bath produced by American inventors and manufacturers the Jacuzzi Brothers. The first Jacuzzi bathtub pump was marketed in 1955 as a hydrotherapy device. In 1968, Roy Jacuzzi created the first all-in-one Jacuzzi bath, which has become synonymous with luxurious bathing.

LEOTARD: A stretchy, close-fitting one-piece garment worn for dance and other athletic endeavors, named for Jules Léotard (1839–1870), a French gymnast.

LEVI'S: Riveted denim jeans, patented in 1873 by Levi Strauss (1830–1902), the purveyor of California gold rush-era dry goods. The brand's famous 501s were named in 1890, for their lot number.

MACADAM: A type of road and highway surface, named for Scottish civil engineer John Loudon McAdam (1756–1836)—not to be confused with John Macadam (1827–1865), a Scottish-born Australian chemist for whom macadamia nuts are named.

SILHOUETTE: A shadow portrait in which a subject is shown in outline only against a contrasting background, named in 1759 for French minister of finance Étienne de Silhouette (1709–1767), in ironic description of his penurious policies.

TEDDY BEAR: A stuffed bear named by toymakers Morris and Rose Michtom for and, indeed, with the express permission of, U.S. president Theodore Roosevelt, after Roosevelt's 1902 refusal to shoot an old, captured bear was popularized in a political cartoon by Clifford Berryman.

TUPPERWARE: Polyethylene storage containers with a unique seal, created in 1946 by Earl Silas Tupper (1907–1983), an American inventor.

ZEPPELIN: A rigid airship, or dirigible, used for both civilian and military transport, patented by German aeronautical pioneer Count Ferdinand von Zeppelin (1838–1917).

When visiting my daughter at Bucknell University, I took note of the fact that it was nestled in the bucolic countryside of Pennsylvania's Wyoming Valley. I knew the name Wyoming was originally Algonquian in origin, but I could track it no further. On my flight back to California, I crossed over the state of Wyoming. Since Central Pennsylvania was settled in the early 1700s; and Wyoming, for the most part, in the middle of the nineteenth century, why would both have the same name? And more to the point, what did this name mean and where did it come from? In this next section you will learn the fascinating origins of the names of all fifty states.

HOW THE STATES GOT THEIR NAMES

ALABAMA: Choctaw for "thicket clearers" or "vegetation gatherers"; also Creek for "tribal town."

ALASKA: Yupik for "great land," "sea-break," or "shore." Russian and British explorers used "Alaska" to refer only to the Aleutian peninsula. After the U.S. purchase, dubbed Seward's Folly, the name was applied to the entire territory.

ARIZONA: Aztec *arizuma*, meaning "silver-bearing"; Tohono O'odham *Aleh-zone* or the Pima *Ali shonak/Arizonac*, which both mean "little, small, or young spring." (Suggested by mining speculator Charles D. Poston.)

ARKANSAS: Algonquian speakers of the Ohio Valley called the native tribes of the area the Arkansas, meaning "[people of the] south wind." In 1881, the state's General Assembly passed a resolution declaring that the state's name should be spelled "Arkansas" but pronounced "Arkansaw." (See *Kansas*.)

CALIFORNIA: From a mythical island, ruled by a Queen Califa, first described in a romantic novel published in 1510 by the Spaniard García Ordóñez de Montavalo. Other suggestions include the Spanish for "hot as an oven" (*cali* = hot, *fornia* = oven, or *fornalia* = furnace).

COLORADO: The word "Colorado" is Spanish for "red," and refers to the muddy Colorado River, or to the red sandstone formations in the area. It was chosen by Congress as the name for the Colorado Territory in 1861.

CONNECTICUT: From the Mohegan *quinnitukqut* or *quonehtacut*, meaning "beside the long (tidal) river."

DELAWARE: From the 3rd Baron de la Warr (Thomas West, 1577–1618), after whom the indigenous tribe, bay, river, and state were named.

Planet California

If California were a free-standing (or should I say free-sliding) nation, it would have one of the world's largest populations of English speakers: about 30 million.

The home of Hollywood (not to mention the rest of L.A. and SoCal), San Francisco, the University of California educational powerhouse (Berserkeley, UCLA, etc.), Silicon (or is it Silicone?) Valley, Stanford, CalTech, Valley Girls, and The O.C., the state automatically magnifies any idea, words, and even phonemes that emanate therefrom. As trackers of words, we really can't ignore California's impact.

QUINTESSENTIAL CALIFORNIA THINKING

We often hear that if California were to be a nation rather than a state, it would be the world's fifth (or sixth) largest economy, right up there with the United States, Japan, Germany, the United Kingdom, and China. What we don't often hear is that if it were a planet, it would be a very strange planet, indeed.

In the California gubernatorial recall election of 2004, in which the Governor (Arnold Schwarzenegger) beat the reigning governor, the election commission "randomized" the alphabet because listing the candidates' surnames by the traditional alphabet was not considered random enough, and thus could theoretically be biased in one candidate's favor.

R, W, Q, O, J, M, V, A, H, B, S, G, Z, X, N, T, C, I, E, K, U, P, D, Y, F, L

Just another day on Planet California. I guess we should think of the state as the early explorers did: Not merely a place, but also a state of mind.

Now let's all sing our RWQs to the "Alphabet Song." Shall we begin?

FLORIDA: From Pascua de Florida, the Feast of Flowers. So named by Ponce de Leon, who discovered the peninsula on either Palm or Easter Sunday in 1513.

GEORGIA: Georgia was named to honor King George II (1683–1760) of England. The colony was established during his reign.

HAWAII: Though Captain Cook named the islands the Sandwich Islands after the Earl of Sandwich, the name did not stick. Hawa'ii might be the name of the traditional home of the Polynesian peoples, with *Hawa* and *'ii* meaning "small (or new) homeland."

IDAHO: Supposedly from the Shoshone term, *idaho*, meaning "the sun comes from the mountains." Scholars, however, have long held that the name was completely apocryphal.

ILLINOIS: From the name of a confederation of six Algonguian-speaking, indigenous tribes, the Illinniwek, meaning "superior men." The confederation included: the Cahokia, the Kaskaskia, the Moingwena, the Michigamea, the Peoria, and the Tamaroa.

INDIANA: Surprisingly enough, from "land of the Indians." Indianapolis, another surprise, is "city of the land of the Indians."

IOWA: From the French transliteration, Ioway, the name for the local Bah-Ko-Je Indian tribe that lived in the area. It means "This is the (beautiful) place." There are several spelling variations in various French documents: Aiouez, Aiaway, Ayaabois, and Yoais. The Spanish added Ajoues; and the English, Ioways.

KANSAS: From Kansas Indians, meaning "people of the south wind." Curiously, the Kansas were relative new-comers to the state, arriving around 1650. (See *Arkansas*.)

KENTUCKY: From any of a number of possible words including:

- a Cherokee word meaning "prairie"
- a Wyandot word meaning "land of tomorrow" (TomorrowLand? Perhaps a Disney pioneer ancestor)
- an Iroquoian word meaning "meadows"
- an Algonquian term for a "river bottom"
- a Shawnee term for the "head of a river"

LOUISIANA: Louisiana, the Land of Louis, was named by the French explorer René-Robert Cavalier, Sieur de La Salle in 1682 in honor of King Louis XIV. He claimed all the land drained by the Missisippi River. Louis XIV, of course, was later beheaded by the guillotine along with his wife, Marie Antoinette.

MAINE: From Maienne, meaning "river of the middle" in French. Before statehood, a number of names were suggested, including New Hampshire, Laconia, New Somerset, Yorkshire, Lygonia, and Columbus. In the end, of course, the surviving name was Maine.

MARYLAND: Named in honor of Henrietta Maria (1609–1669), the queen consort and wife of King Charles I of England.

MASSACHUSETTS: From the Massachusett tribe, meaning "at the Great Hill." Other speculation in-cludes a combination of *massa*, meaning "great," and *wachusett*, "mountain-place."

MICHIGAN: From the French transliteration of the Ojibwa *misshikama*, meaning "big lake," or the Algonquian Chippewa *meicigama*, meaning "big water sea."

MINNESOTA: From a Dakota Sioux Indian word, *mine*, meaning "water." *Minne* appears in numerous place names, such as Minnehaha, Minnetonka, and Minneapolis, which means "cloudy water" or "sky water" and refers to local rivers.

Though Minnesota has been dubbed "the Land of 10,000 Lakes" the number is not accurate. In fact, there are nearly 30,000 bodies of water larger than 10 acres in the state

MISSISSIPPI: From the Chippewa or Ojibwa (or other related Algonquian tongue), meaning "great river," "large river," or "father of waters."

MISSOURI: From the tribe of Sioux Indians of the same name, meaning "muddy water." There are those who prefer "town of the large canoes," "wooden canoe people," or "he of the big canoe."

MONTANA: From the pseudo-Latin, plural form of *montanus*, meaning "mountainous."

NEBRASKA: From the Oto, meaning "flat water or broad river" after the Platte River, which was also called the Nebraska River.

NEVADA: From the Spanish *nevada*, meaning "snowy" or "snow-covered." At various times, Nevada has been called Bullion, Carson Territory, Eastern Slope, Esmeraldo, Oro Plata, Sierra Nevada Territory, and the Washoe Territory.

NEW HAMPSHIRE: From the English county of Hampshire.

NEW JERSEY: From the Isle of Jersey in the English Channel, named Caesarea, after Julius Caesar, who conquered Britain. (After 1500 years, Caesarea had been corrupted into "Jersey.")

NEW MEXICO: From the Spanish name for the territory surrounding the western Rio Grande. In the original Aztec, "*Mexico*" means "place of Mexitli," one of the Aztec gods.

NEW YORK: Originally named New Amsterdam as a Dutch colony. After the British took the state in 1664, it was renamed after the brother of King Charles II, the Duke of York and Albany.

NORTH CAROLINA: Named after Carolus, the Latinized form of Charles I of England. The same goes for South Carolina. The two states were a single colony, Carolina, until divided into "North" and "South" in 1710.

NORTH DAKOTA: From the Dakota Sioux, meaning "friend" or "peace"; originally included the whole of Montana, North Dakota, South Dakota, and Wyoming.

OHIO: The state of Ohio is named after the Ohio River. Ohio is the name that the Iroqois Indians used for the river and means "large river" or "beautiful river."

OKLAHOMA: From two Choctaw Indian words meaning "red people," *okla* and *homma*. Chosen by Allen Wright, the Choctaw nation chief.

OREGON: From the Columbia River, which was at one time called the Oregon or Ouragan, meaning "hurricane" in French. A mapmaker's error also might be a plausible explanation for the name: the Wisconsin River (Ouisiconsink) was misspelled and mismarked, appearing to flow into the Pacific Northwest, the Ouaricon.

PENNSYLVANIA: Penn's Woodlands (woodlands = *sylvania* in Latin), after William Penn, who was granted the state's original charter.

RHODE ISLAND: Named after the Greek Isle of Rhodes, with its Colossus bestriding its harbor, one of the Seven Wonders of the Ancient World.

Not All States Are Actually States.
Vermont was actually a republic, as were California and Texas. Virginia, Kentucky, Pennsylvania, and Massachusetts remain commonwealths.

SOUTH CAROLINA: See North Carolina.

SOUTH DAKOTA: See North Dakota.

TENNESSEE: Of Cherokee origin, from the name of several towns and a major river: Tanasqui. However, its exact meaning has been lost to time.

Alternative Spellings for Tennessee

Tanase, Tanasee, Tanase, Tanesi, Tanisee, Tannasie, Tannassie, Tannessee, Tannassy, Tansai, Tenasi, Tanasqui, Tenesay, Tennassee, Tenesee, Tenessee, Tennecy, Tennesy, Tennisee, Tinnace, Tinassee, Tonice, Tunasse, Tunassee, Tunese, Tunesee, Tunissee, Tunnissee

TEXAS: Derived from the Caddoan language: *tecas* or *tejas*, meaning "friends" or "allies."

UTAH: From the Ute, meaning "people of the mountains." The Apache called the Navajo the Yuttahih, meaning "one that is higher up." Europeans took this to refer to tribes living higher in the mountains.

VERMONT: From the French, *vert mont*, meaning "green mountain."

VIRGINIA: Virginia was named in 1584 in honor of Queen Elizabeth I of England, who was popularly called the "Virgin Queen." Sir Walter Raleigh may have suggested the name.

WASHINGTON: Washington Territory, established in 1853, was named to honor George Washington, the first president of the United States.

WEST VIRGINIA: See Virginia. Until 1861 West Virginia was part of Virginia.

WISCONSIN: Originally, Algonquian for "long river," or a Chippewa/Ojibwa word, *ouisconsin*, meaning "gathering of the waters." (See *Oregon*.)

WYOMING: Derived from the Eastern Delaware
Lenape word meaning "alternating mountains and val-
leys." The geological name for this geography is the
"basin and range," which extends to a part of Utah and
the whole of Nevada. This was the same topography
that was found in the Wyoming Valley in Pennsylvania.

WORDS BEHIND THE MONTHS

The months and the days of the week are named for a variety of
gods and goddesses from the Northern, Roman, and Greek deitific
families. During the French Revolution, the patriots attempted an
entirely new "scientific" calendar consisting of twelve months, each
with three ten-day weeks, each with ten-hour days of one hundred
minutes each. Clearly, it didn't catch on.

JANUARY: Named for the Roman god, Janus, patron of
portals, who was depicted as having two faces: one
looking into the future, and one peering back into the
past.

FEBRUARY: Named after the old Roman purification
ritual, *februum,* which was held midmonth.

MARCH: Named after the god of war, Mars. March was
the first month of the old Roman calendar, which had
only ten months, since winter was apparently considered a "monthless season."

APRIL: Named after the Latin word *aprilis,* meaning
"to open," as nature responded to the warming breezes
of the Mediterranean spring.

MAY: Named most probably after the Greek goddess

Maia. Maia came to be identified with the Roman fertility goddess, Bona Dea, whose festival was during the month.

JUNE: Named after Juno, wife of Jupiter and equivalent to the Greek goddess Hera.

JULY: Originally named Quintilis, the fifth month, its name was changed by Julius Caesar who, of course, named it in his own honor. (He also stole a day from February to ensure that July had the maximum number of days—thirty-one.)

AUGUST: I think you see this one coming Originally named Sextilis (from Latin *sextus* for the number "six"), but changed by the Emperor Augustus in honor of himself. Of course, he also needed to steal a day from February to make sure his month had as many days as that of his predecessor, Julius.

SEPTEMBER: Named from the Latin *septem*, for "seventh," though it is now the ninth month.

OCTOBER: Named from the Latin *octo*, meaning "eight." Though now the tenth month, October was the eighth month in the early Roman calendar.

NOVEMBER: Named from the Latin *novem*, meaning "nine." Though now the eleventh month, November was the ninth month in the early Roman calendar.

DECEMBER: Named from the Latin *decem*, "ten." Though now the twelfth month, December was the tenth month in the early Roman calendar.

THE WORDS BEHIND THE DAYS OF THE WEEK

MONDAY: Named after the Anglo-Saxon *monandaeg*, "moon day," from Mani (Old English, Mona), the Germanic Moon god.

TUESDAY: From Middle English *Twisday*, from Old English *Tiwes doeg*, derived from the Nordic god Tyr (in Old English, Tiw, Tew or Tiu). Tyr was the Northern equivalent of Mars, the Roman god of war.

WEDNESDAY: Named after the Middle English *Wednes dei*, which is from Old English *Wodnes doeg*, meaning "the day of Woden," the king of the Northern gods.

THURSDAY: Named after Thor (Torsday), who was the Northern equivalent of Jupiter or Jove.

FRIDAY: From the Old English *frigedoeg*, meaning "the day of Frige or Frigga," the Northern goddess of beauty, equivalent to the Roman Venus.

SATURDAY: Named after the Roman god of farming and agriculture, Saturn. The Romans called the day *dies Saturni*, "Saturn's day."

SUNDAY: Named simply after the sun, from the Latin *dies solis*, meaning "sun's day" as originated in the Egyptian calendar. The concept was transported to Rome and the rest of Europe over the early years of the first millennium.

CURIOUS HYBRID DOG NAMES

Hollywood celebrities do not have a monopoly on peculiar and attention-getting names for their offspring. There is actually an or-

ganization, the American Canine Hybrid Club, that registers names of new hybrids (two different breeds mated together to produce a new, combined breed). Who knows, some of these names just might end up on the Hollywood children's list in a few years.

COCK-A-MO: American Eskimo–Cocker Spaniel

POOKIMO: American Eskimo–Poodle

PUGGLE: Beagle-Poodle

COCK-A-CHON: Bichon Frise–Cocker Spaniel

WEE-CHON: Bichon Frise–Westie

BULLBOXER: Boxer-Bulldog

RATTLE GRIFFON: Brussels Griffon–Rat Terrier

BULLMATIAN: Bulldog-Dalmatian

CORKIE: Cairn Terrier–Yorkshire Terrier (or Yorkie)

CHIWEENIE: Chihuahua-Dachshund

DOODLE: Dachshund-Poodle

SCHNOODLE: Miniature Schnauzer–Poodle

SNORKIE: Miniature Schnauzer–Yorkshire Terrier (or Yorkie)

PEKE-A-PAP: Papillon-Pekingese

WEE-POO: Poodle-Westie

SHORKIE TZU: Shih Tzu–Yorkshire Terrier (or Yorkie)

TORKIE: Toy Fox Terrier–Yorkshire Terrier (or Yorkie)

The Rook

In the game of chess (in the English-speaking world) the *rook* has the appearance of a castle. *Rook* is another word for "crow," but crows don't look like castles, right? In the High Middle Ages, chess pieces were redesigned from their original forms into something resembling the medieval court: kings, queens, bishops, knights, castles (and pawns). The rook took the form of the castle but kept its original name.

Now what does a crow have to do with chess? Very little. The word *rook* was a transliteration of the Arabic word *rukh*, a giant mythological birdlike creature that you might recall from the Sinbad tales. *Rukhs* were on the board because they were the mortal enemies of the elephant, which were often spotted being carried away in the *rukh*'s massive talons. Elephants on the chessboard? Of course, though we now call them *bishops*. Look closely at the bishop's headdress. Originally, the slit in his ecclesiastical hat was thought to resemble the miter; actually, it was used in earlier times to separate an elephant's ears.

CHAPTER TEN

The Wonders of Language

Certain facts about the evolution of language fascinated me as a young man:

- That the hieroglyphs, or "priestly writing," of the first of ancient Egypt's *eighty* dynasties were incomprehensible to those who would follow in the Middle Kingdom.

- That the great vowel shift of the fifteenth century changed English to such a degree that those who followed, who spoke the "Middle English" of Chaucer, found the earlier version of the language almost impossible to understand.

- That the language now spoken by some 40 percent of the people on this planet was first spoken by a nameless tribe that left absolutely no trace of themselves other than the language we now speak (see the discussion of the Proto-Indo-Europeans in chapter 1, page 19).

Ultimately, questions like these drove my study (and love of) language.

This chapter highlights some aspects of language that I think you will find equally intriguing.

What Objects and Things Did the Original Alphabet Represent?

We can trace nearly all the alphabets ever used from the Phoenician, an early version of the Canaanite script. This Proto-Canaanite alphabet, like its Egyptian hieroglyphic prototype, only represented consonants (termed *abjabs*). It existed around 1400 BC to 1050 BC. After 1050 BC, it was called the Phoenician alphabet. It is the ancestor alphabet to the Greek, Hebrew, Roman, Berber, Thai, and Mongol alphabets.

In some cases, the assigning of sounds to letters can actually make sense to us some three thousand years later. For example, the sound of the letter *M* was the initial sound of the Phoenician word for water. If you look closely at the construction of the letter, you will, indeed, see a physical representation of waves: *MMM* The original sound of the letter *O*, pronounced "en," also sounds like the word for "eye": *oo*. (Perhaps the Phoenicians invented the smiley or emoticon ☺?) But as you'll see below, most of the physical representations of letters are difficult for us to know or understand.

PROTO-CANAANITE LETTERS, NAME OF THE
LETTER, AND OBJECT REPRESENTED

A	alp	"ox"
B	bet	"house"
G	gaml	"throwstick"

D	dalet/digg	"door"/"fish"
E	haw/hll	"window"/"jubilation"
F	aw	"hook"
Z	sen ziqq	"weapon"/"manacle"
H	het	"thread"
I	yad	"arm"
K	kap	"hand"
L	lamd	"cattle goad"
M	mem	"water"
N	nahs/nun	"snake"/"fish"
O	en	"eye"
P	pu/pi't	"mouth"/"corner"
Q	qup	"cord"
R	ra's	"head"
S	sin/sims	"tooth"/"sun"
T	taw	"mark"

Dead Languages

A nifty, if morbid, aspect of the English language is the fact that it is richly endowed from three dead languages—Greek, Latin, and the Anglo-Saxon tongues, each of which lends its particular or peculiar words to everyday speech. This is both good and bad for the cautious speaker of Global English. It's good because it adds to the richness of the language; it's bad because you have to be aware of the idiosyncrasies of each of the contributing languages.

Even though few people outside of academia (or, in the case of

Latin, the Catholic church) speak any of these languages anymore, some of their now-arcane rules of usage still apply.

> *Caution: To assume that dead languages are dead is a grave and dangerous mistake.*

What are the basic criteria for avoiding usage missteps? Well, the first criterion is—did you catch that? criterion (single) and not criteria (plural)—to remember that Global English to a large degree goes back to the Latin and Greek. Think of *alumnus, alumni, and alumnae* (masculine singular, masculine plural, and feminine plural). Confusing, isn't it? Even overtly English terms can be tricky, such as *ox* and *oxen*. But in English these are exceptions, and besides, how many times does the word *oxen* come up in everyday speech? (Apologies to our friends in agribusiness.)

Basically, it's important to remember that both Latin and Greek are *inflected* languages. What this means is that the form of a word carries within itself all sorts of information: it tells you the part of speech, and whether the word is singular or plural, masculine, feminine, or neuter.

THE TWO-MINUTE DEAD LANGUAGE DRILL

To be considered more than simply competent in Global English, you will have to develop a sense of style. Much of this can be accomplished by learning some of the finer nuances of the language that you will encounter in the Two-Minute Dead Language Drill.

Let's start by filling in the blanks. Remember you have two minutes only. Now begin.

SINGULAR	PLURAL
Alumnus	
Curriculum	
	Criteria
	Data
	Kudos
Thesis	
Syllabus	

And for didactic purposes only . . .

Hippopotamus

Rhinoceros

The correct answers are found below.

SINGULAR	PLURAL
Alumnus	Alumni or Alumnae
Curriculum	Curricula
Criterion	Criteria
Datum	Data
Kudos	Kudos
Thesis	Theses
Syllabus	Syllabi

And for the advanced students . . .

| Hippopotamus | Hippopotami (or hippos!) |
| Rhinoceros | Rhinoceroi (ditto for rhinos!) |

Caution: The link between gender and object is not always
intuitively obvious.

Gender, the Politically Correct Use Thereof

Classical languages employ the concept of gender. In postmodern America, this is difficult to comprehend; it's now considered mandatory (excuse me, persondatory or perdaughteratory) to remove all references to gender from civilized communication. (And, yes, there is an elegant and correct way to do this.) The Greeks and Romans, however, had no such qualms. To them, everything was imbued with gender, whether masculine, feminine, or neuter. A ship was female, a rock male, and a datum neuter.

Dead Language Gender is typically way down on the priority list of any aspiring student of Global English. However, it also marks the speaker as an advanced student and one who appreciates the more refined aspects of the language. Sportscasters seem to be aware of this trap. Here's an assignment. To better your dead language skills, spend an afternoon this fall watching, studying, an NFL football (to Americans) telecast. Listen carefully as the announcers introduce the various players and coaches. Listen as they describe former students, sometimes even graduates of those prestigious halls of academe that are also the homes of top-tier college football teams.

They use a single word description, *alum*. An alum is not some sort of nonferrous oxide. An alum is a human being.

If you follow this line of thinking, you'll no longer have to worry about those messy word endings. If sportscasters can transform *alumni* into *alums* in front of millions (and sound almost erudite), why can't you just as deftly transform *curricula* into *currics* and *criteria* into *critters*?

> *Warning: Marks of distinction are words that reveal something about yourself, regardless of your intent.*

Just as certain subtle marks of distinction exist that reveal a fine, discerning mind at work, there are certain words that scream "incompetence." A few examples:

What you said	What you meant to say
irregardless	regardless
infer	imply
affect (as noun)	effect (as noun)
complimentary	complementary
between you and I	between you and me
if I was	if I were

WHAT YOU SHOULD REMEMBER

- *Irregardless* is not proper English (irregardless of what your colleagues think).

- ➤ I infer from your implication (and you don't imply from my inference).

- ➤ A compliment is a compliment but if it's complementary, it is free!

- ➤ Just between you and me, don't use between you and I.

- ➤ If I were in your position, I'd want to show the subtlety of my mind through my command of the subjunctive mood.

Where Did the Question Mark Come From?

Although controversial as to its exact roots, it is generally believed that the origin of the question mark is from the Latin word for question, quæstio. The word was often shortened to Q/o, with the q written above the o. Over time, this was abbreviated to our current symbol for the question mark.

TOP 5 MOST MISSPELLED WORDS

1. *Grateful:* You should be grateful to know that keeping "great" out of *grateful* is great.

2. *Judgement:* This word is governed by one of the rare rules of English orthography. After a *c* or a *g* an *e* can be retained to indicate the letter is "soft," i.e., pronounced like s or j, respectively (though Web users prefer *judgment* to *judgement* by a 3:1 margin).

3. *Its/it's:* The apostrophe marks a contraction of "it is." Something that belongs to it is "its."

4. *Founder:* Flounder is a fish; to founder is to run aground.

5. *Misspell:* You do not want to misspell *misspell.*

OTHER FREQUENTLY MISSPELLED WORDS

All right

Bureau (one of those French-derived spellings that Webster tried to eliminate)

Calendar

Desperate

Embarrass

Facsimile (just use *fax!*)

February

Height

Independent

Ketchup (actually it has multiple spellings)

Library (not the liberry, no matter what they tell you in New Jersey)

Maintenance

Nuclear (in spite of what Presidents Carter and Bush told you)

Occasion

Occurrence

Playwright (means play fabricator or maker; compare copyright)

Precede (and not proceed)

Privilege (you want to add the d to it, don't you)

Questionnaire

Rhythm (no hints for this one)

Schedule

Separate (it's a rat)

Sincerely

Thorough (another francophone spelling)

Truly

Unanimous

Until

Wednesday (Blame it on Wodin, the Northern god)

Xeroscape (desert landscaping, same root as Xerox—dry)

Ypsiliform (just testing to see if you are awake! Shaped like a letter U or upsilon)

You're/Your

Zapata (a drooping mustache)

Zither (the musical instrument played by the wind)

TOP 10 PALINDROMES

Palindrome, the word for "running backward" in Greek, is the term for a word or phrase that reads the same forward or backward.

1. Madam, I'm Adam. (So said Adam to Eve.)

2. Able was I ere I saw Elba. (attributed to Napoleon)

3. Evil did I dwell; lewd I did live.

4. Dogma: I am God.

5. Never odd or even.

6. No trace; not one carton.

7. Go hang a salami; I'm a lasagna hog!

8. Do geese see God?

9. A man, a plan, a canal: Panama. (of Teddy Roosevelt)

10. Are we not drawn onward, we few, drawn onward to new era?

Where Did the Exclamation Mark Come From?

Many historians believe that the exclamation mark got its beginning in Latin origin. The term lo *symbolized joy. The uppercase* I *followed by the lower case* o *seem to have evolved into our present use of the symbol.*

Constructed Languages

Toki Pona is the only known language, constructed or natural, that comes with its own branded symbol. This, in itself, is noteworthy.

Created by Sonja Kisa in 2001 as a way to work through a depressive episode, she created but 120 words, naming the language, in the "native tongue," *good language*. There are now songs and poems and prayers written in Toki Pona. To construct complex thoughts in Toki Pona necessitates the combining of its core vocabulary in interesting and sometimes amusing or even bizarre ways.

Toki Pona is one of the several thousand constructed languages now in existence. Based on Zen-like ideals, the constructed language is now spoken by more than one hundred advocates. Of course, this pales next to the million or more speakers of Esperanto, the artificial language created by Ludwig Lazarus Zamenhof in 1887. Esperanto has grown to a vocabulary of some 75,000 words. It also has spawned many offspring, the most notable, perhaps, is Ido. Ido has been promoted as the international auxiliary language by UNESCO.

SOME CONSTRUCTED LANGUAGES BASED UPON OR HEAVILY INFLUENCED BY LATIN

Achenu	Almalinian	Auxilingua
Adare	Ambarnic	Awolang
Adúlad	Anaqaen	Ayeis
Aeks Nótrï Nódikem	Apralios	Aéstari
	Arcaicam Esperantom	Brandonian
Aenonean		Brujeric
Aercant	Asht	Canis
Aingeljã	Atarel	Carrajena
Aligian	Attrendian	Cilthic

Cni-vcti

Common Romanic

Comunleng

Curco

Daisilingo

Danovën/Arovën

Diallic

Dingwâ

Dodolingi

Dosian

Dununmi

Dutton Speedwords

EDA

Easy Jovian

Egren

Elleya

Esperanto

Europeano

Eùrôpaje

Gilish

Harry Potter Magic Language

Idrani

Illfillin

Inif Xeuivteles

Interlingua

Iqalu

Itlani

Jechoire

Jovian

Juliscan

Kaldon

Kalonese

Kankonian

Karklak

Katiankan

Klaatu's Language

Kor'ekhani

Kot

Kronokayjin

Ksenax

Lahabic

Lanrohidh'il

Latalmish

Latineo

Latinvlo

Lijou

Lingua Internationale

Lingwe Uniwersala

Linka Romànika

Livenia

Logsan

Lúsiaquia

Maerik

Magistri Linguio

Malknarh

Maríshan

Meiko

Mekhael

Melindaran

Mesogeoika

Mhigiwipian

Miricti

Moonshine

Mugdok

Nemeritvie

Neolatino

Neove

New Atlantean

New English

Nu Aves Khara-
Ansha

Nytal

Old Rashurish

Old Sorcery

Omnesian

Oneirien

Onoç

Osceano

Oshorin

Pailodd

Papuash

Patrienish

Platio

Prætiridifin

Quenya

Regelluga

Rigavie Sutanio

Romana

Romanice

Romanico

Romanslavic

Romanze
Standar

Rúvuk

Sasxsek

Satirocitan

SedoNeural

Senáre

Sermo

Shilgne S'drawkab
C'navdair

Silarg

Silindion

Simpekso

Simpla

Sinnish

Spet

Sraelisk

Susachi

Syriculaen

Talossan

Talumena

Tatari Faran

Teonaht

Terpish

Thereskeya

Trurian

Tundrian

Tïsjelán

UberLingua

Un'ky'ok

Ungil

Unish

Utésalañé

Valavya

Varro

Verse

Wenedyk

Yathor

Yeaji

Zdekkite

Zim

Toki Pona is meant to help shape the mind of the speaker, with its simple construction and limited vocabulary in a Zen-like manner. (There are only fourteen speech sounds or phonemes.) This is another example of the Sapir-Whorf hypothesis at work, deliberately so.

Does the language we speak limit our thinking? If this is so, to what extent? And does this call into question the nature of free will, one of the foundational principles of Western civilization?

Listening to a Klingon warrior from *Star Trek* bark out his native commands certainly makes it seem that Klingons are naturally inclined to aggressive behavior. Just as listening to an elf speak J. R. R. Tolkien's Elvish, certainly seems to be a soothing exercise.

Sapir-Whorf Hypothesis

The Sapir-Whorf hypothesis (SWH) is a theory of linguistic determinism, whereby language intersects with thinking, feeling, culture and societal norms. Simply put, you inhabit a language, much as you inhabit a city, state, or country. Language, therefore, helps determine how you interpret and behave in the world.

31337speak

That's right, 31337, is pronounced "leet" as in "feet." Leetspeak is a coded form of written communication on the Internet and in computer games. Taking its name from the word *elite*, it originally designated übergeek status, in terms of both social status and the most accomplished of the group. (The opposite of elite status is that of the newbie or n00b. A newbie is an innocent neophyte; a n00b is an insulting status of vast proportions.) Techies being what they are, *elite* was transformed quickly into *lite* and then *leet* and then *1337, I33t,* and, finally, *31337.* Of course, there is no such thing as *finally* on the Internet. The Net is where you get to watch evolution (or at least natural selection) happen in real time.

Leet is a bit different than the natural languages because Leet is not meant to be spoken, or even pronounced. Composed of alphanumerics and symbols that can be used to represent other alphanumerics and symbols, Leet can be considered a cipher, used to transform plain text into cybertext. For example, the letter *t* can be represented the following ways:

- The number seven: 7

- The plus sign: +

- Two hyphens and a break: -|-

- The number one: 1

- Two brackets and two single quotations signs ']['

- The typographical dagger: †

    . . . and so on.

Other common substitutions include:

    0 for *O* or *D*

    1 for *I, L,* or *T*

    3 for *E* or *B*

    2 for *Z* or *R*

    6 for *B* or *G*

    £ for *L*

All told, there are over 350 characters (letters, numbers, and symbols) in Leetspeak. This provides over one hundred million trillion possible "letter" combinations into possible "words." This should be more than enough to keep the Leet elite industriously occupied for the indefinite future—n00bies beware.

Closing Thoughts

The Future of Global English

The conquest of Global English is nearly complete. It is impossible to hold back this tide. The tsunami of English has already swept over the earth. The question now is how to adjust to this new reality.

I have several suggestions. The first would be to master the language. Yes, acknowledge the sea-change, disassociate yourself from any political misgivings—and get on with it. Global English is here and now—and here to stay. Global English will reside, preside, and thrive. At least in some form.

Here are some possible threads of evolution (or devolution) of the language over the next four hundred years. I chose this perspective because that is the same temporal distance we are from the days of Shakespeare and the King James Bible.

Keeping in mind that the best way to predict the future is to read the past, here are a number of differing scenarios, one of which will be the future of Global English:

1. *The Romanticization of English:* The language devolves into various local dialects that in time become robust

languages in themselves. The precedent for this, of course, is Latin splintering into the Romance languages (Italian, French, Portuguese, Romanian, and Spanish). As Latin is still the official language of the Vatican City state, English will remain spoken in certain enclaves in North Carolina, western Virginia, in the desert Southwest and possibly on a Pacific island or two.

2. *Return to Proto-Indo-European:* Not as outlandish as it might seem, as the green movement decries the technological basis of much of Global English, and back-to-basics promotes the original P-I-E, bereft of millennia of human "progress," as a "green language."

3. *English captured by the Chinese:* The Middle Kingdom strikes back and begins to stake a claim in English language ownership, much as America has done during the last century. The Chinese prove to be excellent caretakers of the language and develop many interesting ways to extend it throughout the Earth and beyond.

4. *Revenge of the nerds—Leetspeak strikes back:* The nerds control the language. All words have dozens of spellings and meanings. Letters, numbers, and symbols intermix. Exposition is heavily encrypted. The precedent: the English language before Noah Webster and the OED. The many variations on Shakespeare's name are mere child's play compared with the near-infinite variety of spellings your children's children will be able to use for their names.

5. *Cyber English:* The robots take control of the language. This form of English would be clipped and very pre-

cise (no fuzzy logic here). Come to think of it, this would be a great leap backward to the time of the King's English, as spoken in, say, Colonial India.

6. *The number of words in the English language will increase a astronomically:* Academics will no longer fret at counting the number of words because the conquest of English will no longer be tainted by political, cultural, and social concerns. Once freed, linguists will count words in the same manner that their scientific colleagues count the number of galaxies, stars and atomic nuclei.

   We will then be able to count *all* the words: every name of every fungus, all the technical jargon, YouthSpeak, all the lishes, everything.

   Dictionaries will no longer be the arbiters of what's a word. Questions of words standing the test of time will be rendered obsolete. Words will bubble forth as a frothy sea-foam of insight and meaning. If a word is used by millions or even thousands of influential elites, regardless of class or any form of identity (gender, ethnic, class, national, or social), it will be deemed a word and recorded for posterity.

7. *There will be no words, only thoughts:* This is a rather difficult scenario to explore, since words all but disappear. Dictionaries will be replaced by something much more ethereal, sort of like a directory of dreams, ideas, and ideals.

   Whatever the future path, this modest branch of Proto-Indo-European that we now call Global English has taken a remarkable journey from a relatively few speakers upon a small "sceptered isle" on the fringes of an empire (who at the time were considered the rankest of barbarians), through the now-hallowed words of Shakespeare and the King James Bible, through those of Austen, Melville, Dickenson, Shaw, Conrad, Churchill, Gandhi, Borges, King, and Nabokov to the present of IMs and txt msgs—and beyond.

Index

Spaghetti westerns,
    24–25
Spanglish, 86–87
Spanish language, 151,
    152–53
Special Effects (FX), 33
Spin, 115
Stargate SG-1, 38
Star Trek, 42, 194
States, names of, 166–75
"Stay the course", 52
Steganography, 131
Stepney, 85
Stewart, Jon, 38–39
Stick Ice, 96
Stog, 95
Storm Surge, 77
Streep, Meryl, 26
String theory, 139–40,
    142
Subpoena, 56
Sun, 91
Sundance, 33
Sunday, 177
Sunset Strip, 33
Superdome, 77
Supermercado, 87
Supersymmetry, 140
Surfear La Internet, 87
Surge, 35, 55
Suri, 44
Survivor, 38, 40
Sutherland, Kiefer, 37
Sweatin', 95
Swenglish, 88
Swift Boats, 54, 61
Swoosh, 125

Ta, 66
Tachyons, 140
Take, 33
Talkie, 31
Teddy Bear, 166
TeleWords, 34–43; recent
    years, 36–39; top 2007,
    34–36; yesteryears,
    40–43
Ten, 138
Tennessee, 173, 174
Terabyte (TB), 134

Terrorists, 62, 69
Texas, 173, 174
Tex-Mex, 87
Textile, 109
Texting (text messages),
    96–98
"That's Hot!", 35
THE, 101
Things Go Better with
    Coke, 121–22
Thingy, 132
Thought Shower, 67
Thousand, 138
Three, 137
Three-Handed Illness,
    83
Three-Peat, 34
Throat Singing, 101
Thursday, 177
Tight, 95
Timberlake, Justin, 39
Timepass, 85
"To Go Where No Man
    Has Gone Before",
    42
Toile, 109
Toki Pona, 190–91, 194
Tonight Show, The, 42
Torus, 140
Trailer, 34
Transformative
    Technologies, 117
Tricked Out, 95
Tricky Dickie, 42
Troca, 87
Tropical Depression, 77
Tropical Storm, 77
Trump, Donald, 37, 38
Truthiness, 36
Tsunami, 38
Tuesday, 177
Tupperware, 166
Tutti-Fruiti Ice Cream,
    41
Twilight Zone, The, 41
Two, 137
Two Americas, 61
Two-Minute Dead
    Language Drill,
    183–85

Understated, 28
Uni, 85
Up Talking, 95
Uranus, satellites, 8
Utah, 174

Van Buren, Martin, 53,
    54
Vatican City, 22
Vegemite, 66
"Verbal Agreement Isn't
    Worth the Paper It's
    Written On", 31
Vermont, 173, 174
Vertical Evac, 77
View, The, 37
Vintage, 109
Viral Marketing, 130
Virginia, 174
Voice over IP (VoIP),
    130
Volkswagon, 126
Voted Off the Island, 40
Vowels, 16–18

Waitron, 68
Wal-Mart, 118
Waltons, The, 41
Wardrobe Malfunction,
    39
Warp and Weft Knits,
    108
Warren G. Harding-ism,
    51
Washington, 174
Washington, George, 53
Wassup (What Up,
    S'up?), 95
Webster, Noah, 15, 198
Webster's, 13–16
Wednesday, 177
Welcomeagain, 82
West Virginia, 174
"Who Are You
    Wearing?", 29
Widdershins, 91
Wikiality, 36
Wisconsin, 174
Wolfe, Tom, 118
Womyn, 67